CONVENTION ON THE RIGHTS OF THE CHILD

Eugeen Verhellen

Convention on the rights of the child

Background, motivation, strategies, main themes

Garant
Leuven-Apeldoorn

First edition: 1994
Second edition: 1997
Third, revised edition: 2000

Eugeen Verhellen
Convention on the rights of the child
Background, motivation, strategies, main themes
Leuven / Apeldoorn
Garant
2000 - Third edition
193 p. - 24 cm
D/2000/5779/96
ISBN 90-441-1081-0

Cover design: Hedwige Dirkx

Garant
Tiensesteenweg 83, 3010 Leuven - Kessel-Lo (Belgium)
Koninginnelaan 96, 7315 EB Apeldoorn (The Netherlands)
e-mail: uitgeverij@garant.be
Also available in Dutch and French

CONTENTS

Foreword 7

Introduction

Chapter 1: **Motivation** 11
1. The historical perspective: changing child-images 11
2. Adultcentrism 19
3. Onthology: children as human beings 19
4. The theory: children are qualitatively not so different 20

Chapter 2: **Strategies** 25
1. The debate on competence 26
2. Trends in the children's rights movement 29
3. Strategies of the children's rights movement 30

Chapter 3: **Recent trends: child-image and the human rights project** 39
1. Child-image and law 39
2. The human rights project 45

Chapter 4: **UN Convention on the rights of the child** 63
1. A short history 63
2. Content of the Convention 76
3. Entry into force and monitoring 81
4. Normative value of the Convention 84
5. Conclusion 86

Chapter 5: **Monitoring** 89
1. Positive sanctioning 90
2. Committee on the Rights of the Child 91
3. The report: an opportunity for pro-active implementation 96

Chapter 6: **Practical consequences of the Convention** 105
1. Education 105
2. Welfare 111
3. Labour 115
4. The media 122

Chapter 7: **Children's rights in the European region** 127
1. The distribution of powers in Europe 128
2. Children's rights in Europe 132
3. Conclusion 142

Epilogue 145

Appendix I: **Declaration of Geneva (1924)** 149

Appendix II: **The United Nations Declaration on the Rights of the Child (1959)** 151

Appendix III: **The Convention on the Rights of the Child** 155

Appendix IV: **Optional protocol to the Convention on the Rights of the Child on the involvement of children in armed conflict** 177

Appendix V: **Optional protocol to the Convention on the Rights of the Child on the sale of children, child prostitution and child pornography** 183

Selected bibliography 191

FOREWORD

The almost universal ratification of the UN Convention on the Rights of the Child, the adoption by the UN General Assembly on May 25, 2000 of two optional protocols to the Convention relating to the involvement of children in armed conflicts and to the sale of children, child prostitution and child pornography, the adoption of the new ILO Convention 182 (1999) on the abolition of the worst forms of child labour which already entered into force on November 2000 and the fact that the constitution of a number of States (South Africa, Poland, Portugal, Slovenia, Belgium) make reference to children's rights, as well as the ongoing discussion on the position of children in society, make it nescessary to revise and to update the initial (1994) and the second edition (1997) of this book.

I hope this third edition again increases the accessibility to the complex phenomenon of children's rights.

I would like to thank my staff members Lieve Cattrijsse, Karl Hanson, Frans Spiesschaert and Tine Vanthuyne for their assistance in the speedy updating of the earlier editions.

Eugeen Verhellen
August 2000.

INTRODUCTION

During the week of November 20th 1999 the tenth anniversary of the children's Rights Convention was celebrated throughout the world.

Indeed the Convention on the Rights of the Child was adopted, without a dessenting vote, by the UN General Assembly on November 20th 1989 (resolution 44/25) exactly 30 years after the adoption of the Declaration of the Rights of the Child, and 10 years after the International Year of the Child.

Less than one year later, it entered into force on September 2nd 1990. At the moment 191 countries have ratified the Convention (Somalia and the United States are the only ones not yet to have done so). This means there is almost universal ratification, which is unique in the history of human rights instruments.

The Convention can be regarded as a historic milestone. On the one hand, it is the culmination of a difficult struggle over decades, aiming at improving children's situation in society, on the other, it is the beginning of a new way of dealing with children, enshrined now in hard law by the international community.

Since the previous turn of the century, the law has reflected our relationship with children, founded on a view of them as creatures who are "not yet" human beings, which has led to them being considered mere objects of the law.

Over the last decades, however, more and more criticism has been levelled at this child-image. Gradually, but with increasing insistence, voices have been heard emphasising that children are in fact first and foremost human beings, and that therefore our relationship with them has to be based on respect for them as human beings. In legal terms this means that children are to be regarded as individuals with fundamental human rights. This new child-image is becoming ever more forceful and hence the present situation has become confused and, at times, even paradoxical. Indeed our relationship with children is still based on the dominant child-image, while, simultaneously, a new one is gaining influence. The Convention on the Rights of the Child reflects this situation.

Children are now formally recognised as bearers of human rights. Enshrining these rights in positive law is however not the end of the matter.

Central to the debate is the relationship between the law and education. Educational science, teaching us how to deal with children, is all about human (children's) rights.

In this book the relationship between education and the human rights project, or specifically the children's rights project, plays a fundamental role.

This book deals specifically with views and theories on children's rights. It contains extensive information on background, motivation, strategies and main trends. It is our intention to use a heuristic structure, allowing the reader to create order from the increasing amount of information received, and to think things through. This makes this book suitable for educational purposes. It provides us with a kind of "common language" which allows us to discuss at a deeper level.

Chapter One deals with motivation, with the different but interconnected reasons for increased attention to the situation of children. It stresses the historical social construction of our child-image.

Chapter Two attempts to describe various strategies for improving children's situation. Here the leitmotif is children's competence, the debate on which is described in some detail.

Our changing child-image obviously has to be examined against the background of wider developments in society. In Chapter Three we take a look at a number of recent trends, emphasising the human rights project and its rapid and far-reaching development, of which our changing child-image forms a part.

Chapter Four is devoted entirely to the Convention on the Rights of the Child, its history, content and monitoring procedure.

Monitoring is also the subject of a separate chapter, Chapter Five, which looks less at formal monitoring models than at quality requirements for effective monitoring.

Because the Convention on the Rights of the Child covers the whole of society and all of its aspects, it seemed appropriate to check its practical applicability in a number of areas, such as education, welfare, child labour and the media. This is dealt with in Chapter Six.

Finally in Chapter Seven we examine the consequences of our changing child-image and of the human rights project in the European Region, concentrating on the tension between human rights and separate children's rights and the way this conflict is handled in Europe.

Chapter 1

MOTIVATION

1. The historical perspective: changing child-images

There have always been children; about this there is no doubt. Attitudes towards them, however, have not always been the same. The changing image of children, shows that children can be treated in different ways. These changes in attitude towards children and in the way we deal with them are consequences not so much of individual, psychological changes in the child but rather of macro-social changes (sociogenesis). This macro-social evolution gradually causes individuals' expectations of others to change. A gradual change in behaviour generated by the dominant expectations will also affect the individual personality (psycho-genesis).

In other words, changing expectations of certain groups of people, such as children, play a crucial role in the way we deal with them and thus also influence child-images. It is therefore important to understand that our image of children is a *social construction, man-made,* flowing from our expectations, and that children are not children *"by nature"*. In fact, regarding children as a *separate social category* is a very recent creation, historically.

Historians, while differing in their views, nevertheless point to various significant approaches to children.

Insight into the social construction of child-images is mainly derived from historical research in the West. The fact that different ways of behaving towards children exist can, however, also be deduced from research into different attitudes to children in different cultures at any given time. Child-images can change through *time* and from *culture to culture.*

1.1. Lack of social awareness of childhood as a separate category

'Indifference' towards children seems to have been the dominant attitude in the West until about the end of the Middle Ages. Infanticide and abandonment of new-born babies were frequent practices in earlier periods of civilisation. In the light of our present-day views on children and sense of propriety, we find many of these practices abhorrent.

History tells us that before the 4th century new-born babies were drowned, left on dunghills, used as bait or sacrificed to the gods during religious rituals. From the 4th to the 13th century it was common practice to abandon unwanted children. Often handicapped children or children who cried a lot were killed. Boys were more valuable than girls. In fact, in Europe this discrimination between boys and girls continued for a long time in the countryside.

For instance, in the 19th century French farmers used to say: "I have no children, only girls". Or the Neapolitan habit of flying a black flag at the birth of a girl in order to tell everyone no congratulations were in order. In those days infanticide and abandonment of children seemed to be considered ordinary methods of family planning.

Also after birth many educational practices were also clear indications of 'indifference' to children. Until the 18th century the majority of new-born children were left in the hands of a wet nurse. Paris police reports (1780) mention 21.000 births: 17.000 were handed over to a wet nurse in the countryside; only 700 were fed by their own mother. And there were other 'educational practices', such as swaddling children, burning them with hot irons to protect them against epilepsy, submerging them in icy water or rolling them in snow to harden or baptise them. Sickness and unhygienic living conditions also caused high infant mortality. Until the 17th century a half to two thirds of all children died before their 20th birthday.

Many historians see high infant mortality (mainly of babies and very young children) as the main reason for the lack of interest in, and even indifference to, childhood as a separate stage of life. It is to be assumed indifference was the best weapon against the horrors of high infant mortality. On the other hand it is also possible adult indifference was the cause of high infant mortality. This seems to have been the case mainly among the better-off. In any case a lack of or very little interest in children was typical of the period, and high infant mortality its consequence (or cause?).

In sum, until the end of the Middle Ages there does not seem to have been any *social awareness* of childhood as a separate category or as a separate social phenomenon.

Children of less than 6 or 7 years of age didn't count, because of high infant mortality. Once the child had survived this period, it became an adult.

As of the age of 7, children took part in the production process. They were trained in the house of a master, where they formed a part of a large community (apprentices - parents relations - servants - maids - visitors). This did not apply to the children of the nobility because they, like their parents, did not participate in the productive process.

Children participated fully in all aspects of life: work - sexuality - life and death. There was almost no difference in treatment between adults and children. In fact the apprentice system remained in existence in the West until well into the 19th century.

1.2. The discovery of the child

It was only as of the 16th century (Rationalism) that people began to take an interest in children. In those days upper-class *boys* began to be 'schooled'. Schools were no longer just technical training establishments for everybody, they became establishments providing a general education, reserved for children.

The moralists (16th-17th century) saw children as 'bad' and education (discipline and training) was meant to make them 'good'. They strongly stressed school and the family.

Romantics like Rousseau and Goethe (18th century), on the other hand, regarded children as 'inherently good'. For this reason they even thought children had to be protected against culture.

Be it in opposite ways, both approaches indicate an interest in children as a *separate group*.

The Enlightenment (18th century), with its belief in the supremacy of Reason, was to bring with it the beginnings of an ideology of progress. In parallel to the development of the natural sciences, the Darwinist view of society reinforced ideas on social progress. The individual was seen as the servant of 'progress', the servant of a society becoming the way it should be. 'The future' being the all-important consideration, present well-being had to be sacrificed more and more to the dictates of the future.

This was certainly the case for children. In this view they were increasingly considered 'the future', 'tomorrow's riches and prosperity', because they had to give shape and form to the prospective 'enlightened' society.

Thus gradually children became a *separate* group with *separate* characteristics, of whom *specific* behaviour was expected.

According to some historians, under the influence of the Enlightenment, two views of mankind gained acceptance: one view, which saw children as creatures yet to be educated, which, provided they were kept sheltered from the world, remained innocent and carefree, thus able to acquire a positive attitude to the world; and another, which saw adults as having an established role in the world, worldly-wise and conscious of their position.

An important historical change came with the transition from a society which did not see the young as a clearly defined group to a society which was interested in defining this group. Furthermore it is to be noted that at the same time, by careful observation, children's specific psychological characteristics were thought to have been discovered. Or one could say with equal justice these hitherto undiscovered characteristics were only then perceived, because it was only then that they occurred, because of a changing social and cultural climate. This process is called the *sociogenesis* of the age group of children: the fact that social changes led to children and adults being regarded as separate groups. Hand in hand with this sociogenetic change there was also the *psychogenetic* development of certain characteristics. Characteristics attributed to children were discovered at a given moment to be child-related and from that time on they were overemphasised in relation to children, which in turn had psychological consequences for children themselves.

Later on, after the discovery of childhood as a separate social phenomenon, there was more differentiation, adolescence, for instance, being regarded a separate age group. This is seen as a consequence of the general introduction of conscription. Thus, the adolescent is a recent social and psychological invention going back only two centuries.

For a long time only the upper classes (the aristocracy and later the upper middle classes) made the distinction. Only much later was it acknowledged by the lower social classes. Originally it only concerned boys. It took a long time before girls were also included in the category of children.

The same development occurred in different spheres of social and cultural life. An example is the emergence of paediatrics. As a medical specialisation, paediatrics only came into existence in the 19th century. It was only in 1872 that the word paediatrics was used for the first time, although an English medical textbook on children had been published as far back as 1554. The following text by a Scottish doctor (1769) is an illustration of the gradual discovery of the child and especially also of the reasons for the discovery.

> "Medicine has paid little attention to the protection of children, out of indifference and failure to recognise what young people have to offer ...Every day every effort is made to keep decrepit, old bodies, on the verge of succumbing, alive for a little while longer, while others who 'later' might be 'useful' to society die in their thousands without anybody bothering to help them, or even to examine them."

The first real *legislation on children* in the West came into existence at the end of the 19th and the beginning of the 20th century. It shows how separate institutions at the same time exclude children from the adult world, and lock them up in their own artificial world, which later on people significantly started calling *youthland*. Because they were powerless against exploitation, children were taken out of the productive process by virtue of special protective measures, put in place, however, not just to protect children, but to serve other purposes as well. Because of a growing sense of the importance of the future and of progress, the development of children started receiving special attention, exemplified by the introduction of legislation on compulsory schooling.

That all of this did not lead to progress for children themselves, despite the ban on child labour on the one hand and compulsory schooling on the other, is demonstrated by the fact that on top of the time spent at school children had to start making extra money to make up for their parents' lost income.

Meanwhile, the 20th century did become the *century of the child* after the book with the same title which was published in 1903 by Swedish author Ellen Key.

These developments are illustrated by an article in an interesting journal, Developmental Psychology Today, which stated that in advanced Western civilisation the process of separation of childhood was now practically complete, but that it was only in the course of this century that it finally spread from the aristocracy and the upper classes to the working classes.

1.3. The present child-image

In this way a new child-image, which to us now seems self-evident, came into existence. Regarding children as a group in their own right, assigning them new status must gradually radically change our relationship with children. In fact, a whole new set of expectations, norms and roles emerged for this newly created social category and ... around the turn of the century all of this was given form in new social institutions (Child protection agencies, paediatrics, systems of compulsory schooling, youth movements, etc.).

According to Skolnick (1983), a number of assumptions about children crept into our Western cultures and were subsequently reinforced:

1) Before they become adults, children go through a number of stages in their development, which differ in quality
2) Throughout these stages in their development children differ qualitatively from adults, e.g.:
   - adults work and are responsible; children play and are irresponsible;
   - adults are rational; children are irrational and emotional;
   - adults think in abstract terms; children think in concrete terms;
   - adults are sexual beings; children are asexual beings;
   - etc.
3) Until they become adults, children have to be separated from adults and spend their time in places which are there to help them become adults (at home, at school with their peers, in 'educational' playing areas). The extent of this quarantine is gradually lessened as children progress through the different stages, but it is only lifted completely when they become adults.

Along with our changing child-image, and its expectations, norms and roles, fundamental changes also gradually begin to occur in our relationship with children, based on the following new educational concept: "Until he/she comes of age (with a limited number of exceptions) a child is immature, and has to be aided and stimulated to become an adult".

In this way children were gradually put in a *position of not yet being*; not yet knowing, not yet being able to; therefore not yet able to express themselves, not yet responsible, ... Their master status became one of *not-yet-being*, their well-being *not-yet-well-being*. Children ended up in limbo, they were put on hold until ...

This is the approach to children, formalised also in law (at the beginning of the century, practically simultaneously, in quite a few Western countries child protection laws and compulsory education were introduced) with which we entered the 20th century. Until then children had been so to speak absent from the law. In the 20th century there have only been marginal changes in the child-image (e.g. the change-over from 'leading' to 'guiding'). In actual fact children were increasingly patronised and their 'stay in limbo' was gradually extended.

1.4. The extension of children's stay in limbo

Although the powerful macro-social momentum towards distinguishing between children and adults caused reactions from the very start, and kept doing so, albeit in a limited fashion, in the 20th century, it would take until the last few decades before more vehement reactions occurred. What had happened? Since the Seventies especially it had become clear that children's stay in limbo was being extended almost uncontrollably. A large number of political measures confirmed and even reinforced it. A number of examples from that time, introduced supposedly in the interests of children, are worthy of note. It is also important to be aware of the introduction of a number of new 'words' to describe this protracted state of childhood: early or late adolescents; young adults; ... the main characteristic in all cases being not-yet-being; in other words dependence.

Postponing their access to the format labour market was a measure considered to be very much in the interests of children. This is made clear by the trend towards extending compulsory education, linking labour market access to part time contracts and/or linking work and training. Strangely enough, all of this happened at a time of economic recession. However since then this trend has continued even in times of economic growth.

Extended periods of ineligibility for unemployment benefits were introduced for the young unemployed. More and more limitations were imposed on their wage and benefit entitlements, and despite all of this youth unemployment levels remained extremely high, paradoxically so, because were young people not told: "do your best, we need you" (by psychologists) or "you are tomorrow's prosperity" (by macro-sociologists). And yet escaping unemployment often meant little more than finding 'temporary refuge' in insecure jobs with dubious legal status. Moreover, the young unemployed had to remain permanently available to the labour market, if they were not to incur serious penalties. Saturation of the labour market, high educational demands, further erosion of their already limited social security coverage, lack of labour law protection, unreasonable rules and regulations, an alienating labour ethos ... all of this in their interests? One could hardly get more cynical. And things weren't and still aren't much better during children's 'extended' education: disillusionment with school, truancy, dropping out, violence, apathy, alcoholism, etc.

And most painful of all was the fact that with the help of the media (in other words quite forcefully) young people were being told they were useless, were not building a future for themselves... Those who were confronted with the problem were also blamed for it, and nobody thought to blame the running wild dynamics behind the extension of children's stay in limbo.

This relationship with the young, which became almost *self-evident,* also had a dangerous side, unprecedented in history. The stay in limbo, stopping young people speaking up for themselves, was not just extended, it broke all *bounds* It was no longer a mere transitional phase (which in the West had lost its ritual character a long time ago) offering hope for the future, it became final, boundless, without hope of change, it became counter-productive.

Now, at the end of the 20th century children are no longer being put in *temporary* storage, very soon there will be no more storage space left for them, or rather for young people there will be *only* storage space. This marginalisation of a whole generation of young people is considered by some to be totally new in our culture. The *superfluous generation*.

It is therefore not surprising that this way of relating to children (our child-image) has negative consequences, which are becoming more and more numerous (and often insoluble). These problems make sombre reading in an increasingly voluminous book, a black book which still takes courage to read but which in itself will be a very good argument for efforts to be made to change our relationship with children.

We know our child-image is a social construction. Our relationship with children is not imposed by nature and can be changed. Not only can it be changed, but in the light of what has preceded, it needs to be changed.

Amongst other things, educational efforts in this direction are being undertaken. However, educators traditionally target their work mainly at the micro-level. However well-intentioned and praiseworthy efforts at this level may be, there is a clear risk of discouragement. Progress achieved by these efforts stops at the door of the classroom. They are no more than a drop in the ocean. Which is not to say we should not respect and encourage this sort of micro-level work which in fact is often heroic and shows deep respect for children.

However, it is history itself which teaches us that this sort of work always has to be carried out in the knowledge that our relationship with children has its roots not so much at the individual but at the structural level. Because of the lessons taught to us by history, educators should urgently and intensely start tackling this level.

2. Adultcentrism

There is a recurring risk that the debate on the extension of children's stay in limbo will be conducted in a vacuum ("after all young people are not children"). There is, however, no denying the direct link with the social construction of the whole child-image and the causative dynamics of power behind it. In fact, apart from a number of known elements of these dynamics of power, children also appear to be the victims of another dynamic influence: adultcentrism, the exaggerated egocentrism of adults. So far much too little attention has been paid to this particular influence, and, most importantly, to the interaction between different dynamic influences.

The negative consequences of man's (especially Western man's) ambitious *anthropocentrism* (man as the centre of the world), are becoming increasingly visible. Furthermore Western history so far has known a number of dark eras, caused by merciless *ethnocentrism*. We only have to look at the relationship between the Northern hemisphere and the Third World. *Macho* attitudes in their turn keeps half the population away from power.

Our relationship with the younger generation, however, remained immune to change for a long time. And all the while, because of *adultcentrism*, a sizeable proportion of the population was made subservient to the rest. And yet the justification for this dominance of children by adults is extremely tenuous. Adults exercise their power solely as a direct consequence of very specific duties: they have to protect and raise their children, who, being biologically immature, need care and assistance. That is all. Notwithstanding this we know that, in combination with ethnocentrism, there is even gross dereliction of these primary duties with regard to Third World children (food, clothes, health care, ...). And where we live too the consequences of adultcentrism are clearly similar in nature (e.g. child abuse).

In other words, there is evidently a lot wrong with our interpretation of the primary duty to "raise children" and of the concept "child".

3. Onthology: children as human beings

In our daily life there are many different examples of socially-created dependence of children. For instance, it is taken as read that children are to be regarded as objects, as 'goods', and as 'property of'... This is also clearly reflected in law. Children have no rights, as demonstrated by the Universal Declaration of Human Rights in which age is not regarded as a criterion for non-discrimination. It is therefore not surprising that a number of fundamental rights in the Declaration are denied to children.

And the fact of the matter is, quite simply: children are human beings! Therefore children are entitled to the same rights as all other human beings. Children do not need to be given rights, they have them.

Sometimes it is suggested that children are different because they are unfinished products. But in actual fact every human being is an unfinished product. And this being unfinished, in different degrees, is the source of creativity, communication at the most profound level, interdependence, culture,... There are endless numbers of differences between people: sexual, ethnic, age differences ... And none of these differences legitimises unequal treatment.

On top of all this, like other groups, children have a number of specific rights, because of their biological immaturity. These preferential rights are sometimes called protective rights.

Educational theory, which tells us what our relationship with children should be, has the job of guaranteeing and protecting both children's fundamental and their preferential rights. This is a moral imperative. In other words educational theory is first and foremost a matter of human rights.

4. The theory: children are qualitatively not so different

The dominance of the positivistic scientific ideal, which has come about over the years, resulted among other things in the child becoming a research object rather than subject (sometimes children are not involved at all). The hypothetical deductive method used involves fragmentation of the object studied (into, inter alia, cognitive, emotional, moral and physical aspects), and its isolation from the larger group.

In this way, children have come to be viewed more and more as *separate* beings, to be distinguished from adults.

This scientific approach is still being used and continues to dissect the differences between children and adults and amongst children, without worrying too much about ideological and social references, thus in theory unbiased and objective.

In this way children and adults end up in a vicious circle: because of the differences brought to light children are treated differently from adults, which reinforces the differences, and so on, and so on ...

It is however possible that the child-image so constructed does not correspond to what children really are. Children having been research object rather than subject, there was much more likelihood of their frame of reference being ignored, pushed aside, indeed repressed, and of their way of giving meaning to themselves and the world remaining hidden.

In so far as the specific nature of children is recognised, it is considered inferior. What children really are has become a closed book, a *black-box*, which because of the sustained stereotyping described above, is almost bound to remain sealed. The box of Pandora?

However there were and still are other scientific perspectives which lead to completely different insights and therefore different conclusions about our relationship with children. In the present state of play in science, the interactionist approach helps to clarify matters. In fact, symbolic interactionism explains the evolution and meaning of a number of life's fundamental processes. Man, and also the child, are described as "meaning-makers", as essentially actors, rather than reactors. Thus, we are taught, people see their surroundings very selectively (the process of "indication"), they see only that which is to do with their own interests. Interactionism is a pragmatic attempt to explain among other things why people notice certain phenomena and not others. Children use the process of "indication" in the same way as adults. And yet, while "indication" is an unalienable right of children and adults alike, the freedom to use it probably is firmly repressed in children from an early age, making adults lose sight very quickly of what is important to children.

The next step is somewhat more complex: it is the process of giving meaning, of interpretation. People give a meaning to those phenomena they indicate, a meaning which they choose out of many different meanings, and which again coincides with their interests. This process of interpretation is typically human. People do it all the time. Children also do it all the time. It is their unalienable right. And this brings us closer to the roots of the repressive mechanism. Some interpretations of a given phenomenon seem to be considered more important and therefore have a better chance of becoming dominant, without in fact being better.

Through more complex processes of interaction between people, and between people and objects, people create a self-image, an identity. The self is the ever-developing ability we have to find answers to questions like: who am I, why am I who I am, ...? It is the human capacity to have a view of oneself. The way we see ourselves and judge ourselves depends largely on how we interpret other people's response to us. To do this people, and therefore also children, use a technique of getting out of themselves (cf. Romanticism), called "role-taking". This is how we obtain a view of ourselves as others see us. We manage this by placing ourselves in other people's position. And by assuming other people's view of ourselves, we develop our own identity.

Essentially this is an interactionist process. We step into other people's shoes and try to look at ourselves the way they do. In other words, the self is determined by interaction, by the way we act, every action being pragmatic, taken to further our own interests, to achieve our own objectives.

At first the self is quite diffuse. Through different stages of development it becomes more organised. The process of role-taking, which occurs at first only with significant others in specific situations, later on also occurs in situations which involve several people. Then we have to put ourselves in the position of several people and take several roles. Our actions are no longer only determined by the "specific other", but by the "generalised other". This way values, norms and meanings are interiorised.

So to a large extent the self is a social creation, which determines our own standpoint, expectations, and intentions through interaction with specific others and with the generalised other. The process of role-taking results in a response which should be seen as one of many possible responses to the expectations of others. This is partly the consequence of the afore-mentioned important intermediary processes of indication (through which we notice certain elements in a situation because they are important to us) and interpretation (through which we give a certain meaning, of importance to us, to these selected elements).

People, and therefore also children, are seen as *meaning-makers*, as essentially actors and not just as reactors. Furthermore the individual does not just use other people as points of reference, he is also influenced by his perception of the role he wants to play (role-making). Because role-taking and role-making go hand in hand, interactive processes become to a certain extent autonomous, they run their own course and follow their own logic. They are characterised by their "Einmaligkeit", which means that behaviour is not necessarily objectively recognisable from the outside (as mainstream scientific perspectives claim).

Interactionism sees society as changeable and pluralistic, rather than static. Social order is created through role-taking. This is what the generalised other refers to. Significant symbols shared by several people form a reference to a *"working consensus"*, a consensus produced by a never-ending process of negotiation. This leads to a "negotiated order", the result of interactive situations in which the participants, through mutual concessions, try to bring about a manageable definition of a given situation. Therefore the basis of the social order constantly has to be reconstructed by the participants in the interaction. Thus the emphasis is placed on changeability and diversity in society, rather than on the assumption of a *generalised consensus*.

It flows from all of this that interactive processes are also attempts to convince others to accept one's own definition (those elements noted, and our interpretation of them) of a situation, and of everybody's role in it. This is why interactive processes have to be considered inherently conflictual. The partners in the interaction, using the means at their disposal, develop strategies to impose their own definitions on each other. Each interaction therefore involves a range of interests (Even lack of interest is an interest). One person's interests are not another's. *Power* therefore plays an essential part in interactions. Hence the danger of repression is very real, and because of adultcentrism, for children it is even greater.

These problems of definition have received extra attention in interactionism. We have for instance Thomas's interesting principle: "If men define situations as real, they are real in their consequences". In other words, people live and work in many situations, which are constantly changing and which are defined by them as real and therefore acted upon, which makes them real.

It goes without saying that if adults, who have the necessary power, continue to consider their meanings as dominant, they not only seriously affect the individual identity of the child by giving it little or no opportunity to make its own meaning (or at least by considering the child's meaning inferior), but also, and this is as much of a problem, define one particular child-image as real, this child-image slowly becoming embedded in social institutions and structures and becoming part of *social reality*.

It has been demonstrated above that what we call social reality is in fact a social construction, that, in other words, through the interaction between people and during this interaction behaviour is given meaning. Typifications emerge because behaviour becomes routine and starts following a certain pattern. Such routine actions, which reappear also in language, gain certain objective meanings. In this way, social reality is objectivised in language, objects and institutions, which reflect our common stock of knowledge about reality. Our actions appear to follow a predefined structure, and we seem to live in a fixed reality (e.g. our relationship with children).

Everybody seems to behave in the same way with regard to this reality. They appear to be giving it the same meaning: it becomes *the* reality, it becomes *common sense*. Because of this complex objectivising mechanism we lose track of the fact that this reality has been constructed by us over the years, that it is a human creation. And therefore we also overlook that fact that, despite the existence of this reality, the creative process still continues.

By using certain meanings (rather than any of the many others) to define situations we immediately attribute positions, which because of the above-mentioned objectivising dynamic, appear natural, self-evident and unchangeable.

Situations are defined, and positions attributed, whereupon form and content of present and future interactions (and even past ones, which causes one-sided retroactive interpretations of history in the style of: "it has always been like this") are determined, legitimised and become reality.

Children, and the position attributed to them, are such a historical creation.

Especially through the discussions on *"participation"* of children, based on their *intrinsic* quality as meaning-makers, it becomes clear how the once assigned position of children is questionable. For the actual "common sense" is telling us that children are no-yets, having not-yet an opinion, so being not-yet meaning-makers. They have to learn to become so.

Therefor participation of children is still dominantly regarded from an *instrumental* point of view, even as a tool: participate to learn how to participate and by learning so becoming a good adult citizen.

Chapter 2

STRATEGIES

The status of children as it evolved was marked by the absence of practically all civil rights. There is no philosophical or legal recognition of children's right to self-determination. They are essentially powerless: they have no control over their own lives, a marked characteristic of slavery.

It is therefore not surprising that children's status increasingly came to be perceived as a problem, by different people from different fields. This diversity led directly to the so called "children's rights movement". This means that the dominant image of the child finds itself in a process of *deconstruction* and *re-construction*. This transitional phase has already lasted for several decades.

The children's rights movement wants the full, fundamental civil rights for children to be acknowledged, and children to be entitled to exercise these fundamental civil rights autonomously. The recognition of children's autonomy and right to self-determination is fundamental, as is the acknowledgement of their legal capacity.

Equal rights, unaffected by age, are not so much the *objective* as the *starting point* of the movement. It does not want identical treatment of children and adults (assimilation), it wants children to have the guarantee that they can be themselves. It considers it important for the needs, interests and qualities of children to be recognised, and not to be sacrificed to the interests of others.

At the moment it is common practice in our society to remove children from situations which are dangerous for them or in which their needs cannot be satisfied, rather than to change the situations themselves or provide the necessary means to satisfy their needs. This practice must change, if we are not to go on infringing children's right to freedom and their rights as people. The children's rights movement is convinced that the liberation of children will have a liberating effect on all members of society. Therefore it is of the opinion that it is urgent for us to do away with the present-day division of different age groups into different worlds.

The children's rights movement also argues for children's right to participate in the shaping of their own living conditions, and of society. For this they have to be given equal access (distributive justice) to the necessary resources and structures.

The right to participate in democratic decision-making, the right to self-determination, and the right to exercise these rights autonomously are fundamental human rights. *Human rights* are therefore an important point of reference for the children's rights movement.

Some people think that recognition of the validity of human rights specifically for children does not conflict with the ambition of the children's rights movement to meet the special needs of children but is in fact complementary to it. They do feel however that it is necessary to translate the specific needs of children into preferential rights. Here the Declaration on the Rights of the Child (1959) played an important role. The UN General Assembly adopted the Convention on the Rights of the Child 40 years after the Declaration on Human Rights, and this was expected to contribute a good deal to enforcement of children's rights. In any event, a certain amount of protection is considered necessary if children are not to be exploited by unscrupulous individuals, organisations and states. Protection should not be achieved by denying children the right to make their own choices, but by accompanying children's freedom of choice with care and attention to the alternatives offered to them, and among other things by preventing coercion or exploitation based on age. There is nothing wrong with protection in itself: everybody needs some protection from something. A protection system based just on age is however considered objectionable, since such a system takes no account of what the individuals can do, and therefore often causes more harm than good.

Categorising problems is a direct cause of these negative effects. It is not only children, but also adults (e.g. the elderly) who are victims of society's obsession with this approach to solving problems by putting them into age categories.

1. The debate on competence

The ideological and scientific debate on children's rights has, though, taken place mostly at a more pragmatically level. Lately there has been broad consensus on the recognition of (material) rights. There was still little talk particularly in the Seventies about children having the same individual rights, the same human rights as other people. On the other hand there was a lot of argument about whether children should be considered able to exercise these rights, whether in other words they should be entitled to exercise these rights autonomously. Formal rights therefore, i.e. the right to exercise substantive rights independently. The central notion in this debate being *competence.*

Indeed the most fundamental, recurring argument against autonomous rights for children is their supposed incompetence to take well-founded decisions. According to this view children are not sufficiently mature physically, intellectually and emotionally and they lack the necessary experience to make a rational judgement on what is and is not in their interest.

The children's rights movement has made every effort to counter the arguments supporting the theory of incompetence, by disputing their validity, relevance and soundness.

Since 'competence' is not considered a valid argument when applied to adults, its *validity* when applied to children is also questioned. Even when adults are "incompetent" in certain areas, there is still an assumption of potential competence. If this reasoning is applied to children, there is clearly no reason to consider them inferior to adults. The question then has to be, even if we are dealing with competence which still has to develop or be acquired, what is the more morally appropriate choice: freedom or inferiority?

There has been little research in this field, but it shows that knowing one has choices (in other words self-determination) results in heightened awareness of one's own power and influence. Moral development is improved, and adapting to conventions is easier. There is less recalcitrance, and motivation is enhanced. According to some, from a purely utilitarian point of view, the advantages of treating children as fully-fledged persons clearly outweigh the disadvantages of possible 'bad' decisions being made by immature children.

The *relevance* of the arguments supporting the incompetence theory is also disputed by the children's rights movement, because official recognition of a human being as a fully-fledged individual does not in any way coincide with that individual reaching full maturity. Here reference is made to the fact that the time spent as an adolescent continues to lengthen, as does children's stay in limbo.

And finally the *soundness* of the incompetence arguments is also contested. They could perhaps be considered sound when dealing with very young children. But if they are really incompetent to exercise their rights, there should not be any problem in acknowledging them, since they will not exercise them anyway. And surely this cannot be a reason to deny them the right to be consulted and informed on important decisions concerning them and to be represented in situations where their interests may differ from those of adults. The children's rights movement does not just use counter-arguments, it also makes a positive case for children's competence. Since the time of Jean Piaget's experiments it has been known that at a very early age children already have basic intellectual and moral capacities and that from the age of 12 they are certainly capable of making complex decisions. From that age onwards at least there is in fact very little qualitative difference between children and adults. Moreover observation of ordinary daily situations outside the laboratory reveals that there is a lot more to be said for children's competence than has generally and traditionally been assumed in literature. Furthermore it appears that adults too are also only capable of functioning at optimum moral and cognitive levels in situations with which they are very familiar.

Children have been shown to be psychologically much more articulate than is generally thought. Both physically and socially they have been shown to be able to survive much earlier than expected.

In daily life they appear to have more resilience, strength and perseverance than was thought 'theoretically' possible. This has been shown in war situations or during disasters. In literature we find descriptions of independent communities of children, which came into being not so long ago during natural disasters or civil wars. On the basis of this sort of information some people are of the opinion that protecting children is an unnecessary luxury.

Nowadays and in less extreme situations, children have turned out in practice to be well able to make important contributions to society. They work, are conscripted, give birth to and raise children and look after younger children and older members of the family. Although they do all this in less than optimum circumstances, they seem to manage reasonably well. Even everyday legal transactions (e.g. buying and selling) provide us with arguments to support the case for children's competence.

Since it is sufficiently documented, it is even more regrettable that children are still not studied and regarded as fully-fledged partners in society. Because, once again, what children know, what they are capable of and what they are remains a mystery. This is why the arguments for incompetence continue to dominate the debate.

In fact the outcome of the debate on competence ought to be that it is essential that children's right to self-determination be recognised *in order to* make them more competent and not the other way around: that their right to self-determination be (gradually) recognised because (step by step) they have gained more competence.

2. Trends in the children's rights movement

The above may give the impression that the children's rights movement is a monolithic bloc. In actual fact there is a whole range of opinions. There are a number of trends deriving from the position taken in the debate on competence.

2.1. The reformist trend

First of all there is a trend which regards the arguments in favour of incompetence as valid, but is of the opinion that our society seriously underestimates children's capacity to take well-founded, rational decisions. The supporters of this view feel children acquire this capacity much younger than is generally assumed, and that this capacity is gradually acquired. Hence they argue in favour of lowering the age of majority and of the gradual acquisition of rights by children.

2.2. The radical trend

The children's liberationists, on the other hand, dispute the validity of the incompetence arguments on moral grounds; their basic principle (the highest moral standard) is equality of all people. Any form of discrimination, including therefore discrimination on the basis of age, is considered morally wrong. It is considered that the only possible solution is the acknowledgement of full human and civil rights, for children too.

2.3. The pragmatic trend

A third trend is increasing in importance. Supporters of this trend wonder why it would not be possible, in practice, to acknowledge children's full civil rights, including the right to exercise them autonomously, unless it can be proven they are incompetent to exercise certain rights, and there is general agreement on this ("children have all rights unless..."). Experience with adults shows this is perfectly possible. The main advantage compared to the present situation would be that the burden of proof is reversed. At the moment children are in a much weaker position because the burden of proof lies with them. They have to demonstrate they are entitled to self-determination ("children have no rights unless ..."). This is the reason why for children many rights become obligations (e.g. the right to schooling = compulsory schooling). This pragmatic trend becomes more and more visible in national and international jurisdiction (cf. infra).

3. Strategies of the children's rights movement

To achieve it's objectives, the children's rights movement employs four main strategies.

3.1. Child-advocacy

The most important strategy is child-advocacy. Child-advocacy aims at changing systems, institutions and legislation in our society in order to increase children's opportunities for self-determination. Its actions are often directed the ways in which society creates conditions which limit or adversely affect the opportunities available to children. From this perspective, efforts to help individual children, however wide-ranging, will not change anything. What is needed is structural change; this is the objective of child-advocacy. Child-advocacy in this form is a key notion in the children's rights movement. It has also been given the name ombudswork.

Within this strategy there are two distinct models.
First of all there is the Scandinavian model, in which the authorities consider it their task to improve children's role in society and how they function in it. A remarkable example is the "children's ombudsman" instituted by the Norwegian parliament in 1981. Within the Norwegian system, which covering both the public and private sector, individual complaints can lead to fundamental steps to improve the position of children. In the meantime, this Norwegian model has clearly inspired other initiatives all over the world, whereby efforts are made towards installing ombudsmen for children. Ombudsmen for Children Offices or similar institutions, on national, state or city level, were esta-

blished in about twinty countries: Australia, Austria, Belgium, Canada, Costa Rica, Denmark, Finland, Germany, Guatemala, Iceland, Israel, Luxembourg, New Zealand, Norway, Peru, Portugal, Russia, Spain, Sweden, Ukraine,...
For the European region, supported by Unicef Europe, a *European Network of Ombudspersons for Children* (ENOC) is operating since 1996.

The Anglo-Saxon model is the second form of organised child-advocacy. Here the driving force comes from private organisations, rather than the authorities. Sometimes a special kind of action is used in this model, called "class-action-litigation". An important part of advocacy activities in the USA takes this form. This is an action in which a small group of plaintiffs challenge a practice, a policy or legislation which concerns not only them, but a whole group of people in the same situation. When a case is recognised as a class-action (i.e. when it meets a number of strict requirements), the verdict of the court becomes applied to all members of that class. Among other things, the universal right to education, including the severely handicapped, and the duty of the authorities to provide it, are to a considerable degree the result of class-actions. This form of action is therefore used by the Children's Defence Fund, the most important, nation-wide child-advocacy organisation in the USA, set up in 1973. The way this organisation functions is exemplary for this child-advocacy model. The Children' Defence Fund works on the following principles. First of all child-advocacy is considered a specialised occupation. The Fund looks for specific problems which seriously affect large numbers of children, and concern subjects which can lead to broad institutional changes. Different strategies (information campaigns, case-files on abuses, policy advice, support for local initiatives, court cases) are used, aimed at different levels of society (local, regional or national). Sound child-advocacy requires careful preparation, stamina and adequate follow-up.

Very soon the concept of child-advocacy became known outside the children's rights movement and was ascribed new meanings: ordinary provision of services and efforts on behalf of individual children also came to be known as child-advocacy.

Although this sometimes made it difficult to distinguish between a well-meant desire to protect children and genuine child-advocacy, the redefinition of the concept did mean that new objectives evolved.

Because of children's (economic) dependence, because of their essentially passive legal status, child-advocacy has to provide children and young people with access to the opportunities, services and protection they are entitled to as citizens. Other initiatives have been aimed at supporting children in their quest for justice.

Attention is also directed to the relationship between children and facilities provided for them, to make services on offer a better response to their needs. These needs can be expressed as rights, so that the rights are recognised, made law and applied in practice.

Sometimes child-advocacy concentrates on specific themes, and a specific approach is selected with the broader objective of improving the position of children in society. A range of initiatives in the field of children's rights have emerged.

One of them is a Dutch initiative originating in Amsterdam in 1985: the "Children's rights shops". Also in Flanders two shops are established. The aim of the Children's rights shops is to provide information, guidance and actual legal assistance to children. The Children's rights shops consider it their task to give advice on the legal position of children to children, to educators and to people and bodies involved with children. Through their work, the Children's rights shops seek to promote recognition of minors as people with legal rights, and draw attention to the way they view the world.

In French speaking Belgium the "Services Droits des Jeunes" give legal aid to young people and their families. They emphasise recognition of young people's independence, as well as prevention and assistance in cases of social exclusion. They use the law as an instrument. The organisation acts at the request of a young person or his family, without having to justify itself to any third party (magistrate, police, social services). The young person and his family alone decide on the objectives to be achieved and the means to be used.

Another example is the "Japanese Federation of Bar Associations" which carries out innovative work in the human rights sector. The association will, for instance, appoint a lawyer specialised in child protection legislation to assist a minor involved in a court case. The aim of the program is to defend the human rights of minors.

3.2. Study of the child (ethnography)

The children's rights movement is becoming more and more aware of the need to understand the ideas, desires, wishes and thoughts of children (the child as "meaning-maker"), of which so far we know very little.

If children's socialisation is regarded as a process of learning to become an adult, of adaptation to society, then research will only look into what the child is and does in its daily existence in so far as this is relevant to the educational objectives. Only when researchers learn to understand the world of the child as the child sees it, will they be able to contribute to a framework of children's rights, meeting both the needs of children and those of society. This is why many people feel that studying the child's perspective is the most valuable contribution which can be made to the conceptual development of a children's rights structure.

While this sort of research is still in its infancy, some efforts have been made. One example is a Dutch study (Pedagogiek op je knieën - Education on your knees) by Bleeker and Mulderij into children's perception of their environment. The following principles were used: recognising children's perception of here and now (their present existence), trying to understand conditions determining their development (children's future existence), and recognising equality between children and adults.

The study organised by the Belgian UNICEF committee for the campaign "Children's wishes become children's rights" is also worthy of note. The campaign's aim was, on the one hand, to give all Belgians under the age of majority an opportunity to call upon the government to ratify the UN Convention on the Rights of the Child as soon as possible and, on the other hand, to allow children to express their view on the Convention in the form of writing or drawings. These were subsequently used to study children's perspective on their rights.

The European research project called *Children on the Family* (1995), carried out by J. Van Gils, is intended to provide a survey of the child's point of view. Children are given the opportunity to express the way they experience their most important life environment, their family.
This sort of study, in which the greatest concern is *'how do children get to express themselves?'* takes a step in this direction by involving the child as a subject in the research.

It is also necessary to study children as a social category. So far they have been studied mainly from a psychological and educational point of view. We must however also look at children as a separate section of the population from a structural viewpoint.

Arlene Skolnick does exactly this in her work on the construction of the separate social category i.e. the child, in which she gives a historical overview of how our present view of the child, with its own psychological characteristics and separate institutions, has come about.

Pioneering work on children as a separate social category was undertaken by the European Centre for Social Welfare Policy and Research in their study "Childhood as a social phenomenon." This sociological study of different countries examines children as a historically and culturally changing group (called "childhood"), children are being regarded as a social construction and a permanent structural factor in society and not only as "the future generation".

Children as a social class are integrated in society in that they participate in organised activities. They are part of a social structure, and as a social group interact in different ways with other groups, the idea being that there is a general social framework which is essential to all social groups. It is assumed, then that there are forces in society which influence different social groups in different ways. In other words the study looks into social phenomena which exert a dynamic influence on the creation and reconstruction of children as a social category. Precondition for understanding children's perception of their own situation is freeing them of adult-centred categorisation and giving them conceptual autonomy. Serious efforts are therefore made in the project to investigate children's activities as phenomena with their own intrinsic value. This international exploratory study looks into children's sociography, children's activities (in school, at home, ...), distributive justice (are economic, social and cultural means fairly distributed over the different generations), children's economic interests and finally their legal status.

3.3. Children's self-organisation

The children's rights movement is of the opinion that so far too much attention has been directed at specific problems of specific groups of children, and that it is necessary to stress the pool of experience common to all children, as we can understand it from an examination of children's status in our society. Emphasising children's common interests would make it possible for children themselves to join forces (self-organisation) in order to bring about the structural changes aimed for. Looked at in this way, participation is here an instrument for the achievement of external objectives: this is participation as a function. On the other hand, participation also has an inherent value, an end in itself.

It is precisely in the ability to *take part in*, to *belong*, that human dignity lies, including that of children. This is itself one of the most structural changes the children's rights movement wishes to achieve.

This view has led to several initiatives with varying degrees of self-organisation by children.

NAT's (Niños, Niñas y Adelescentes Trabajadores), a (self-)organisation of working children is strenuously active to obtain better working conditions and to have recognised the right to freedom (and support) of association (even as a formel partner in the debate on child labour, for instance on drafting national and international ILO rules). This gives really a major change at the childlabour-discussion, since up to then this was only focussing on the abolishment of child labour.

The French organisation "Association Nationale des Conseils d'Enfants et de Jeunes" is one of them. Its objective is to bring together people and initiatives aimed at producing a permanent structure to promote recognition of children and young people as fully fledged partners in the local community, an objective which corresponds to general thinking on children's status against the background of the Convention on the Rights of the Child. Children's City Councils are just such a permanent structure for participation and dialogue, enabling an exchange of views between young people and their local authority to take place. Through the Children's City Councils adults are brought face to face with the view of children and young people, and forced them to adapt their own views. Children are no longer regarded only as tomorrow's adults, but also as today's fully fledged interlocutors, with their own place in society to which they are fully entitled. The members of the Councils are elected in schools and youth clubs. Their proposals and their criticisms may be about town planning, road safety, leisure activities, social problems in the city, school, anxiety about future jobs, cultural matters, ... Numerous proposals on council policy are made by children elected onto City Councils.

In 1995 *Youth Planet, The European Association of Children Councils,* was established.

An example in the media is the children's press agency "Children's Express" in the United States and the U.K. Children cover events, conduct interviews, write articles which are submitted to the "adult" press: local newspapers, international magazines, television, ... Through these channels children's interests and their views are aired in the media, which is regarded as a vital link between the public, policy makers and children.

Specific attention should be given to the *"What do You Think"*-project. It is an international initiative initiated by Unicef at the occasion of the 10th anniversary of the Convention on the Rights of the Child. It was initiated in 12 pilot countries: Belgium, Germany, Italy, Mali, Mexico, Philippines, Romania, South Africa, Spain, Switzerland, the United Kingdom and Vietnam.

Based on article 12 of the Convention the initiative aims to create and enhance possibilities for children to express their views and for them to propose ways of improving respect for their rights more specifically through the *reporting process* on the implementation of the Convention (see chapter 5).

3.4. Networking

Finally, putting people and organisations in touch with each other is also considered a priority. Very often people and organisations are active at different levels and in a variety of fields, trying to generate social change in relative isolation, while their objectives are closely related. First we have to mention the international conferences on Ombudswork for children (Gent: 1989, Amsterdam: 1992). The main objective of these conferences was to determine motivation and strategies to be used to promote children's human rights. Along the same lines, we have the scientific research networks, such as the Belgian Children's Rights group, set up after the Gent Conference on ombudswork for Children. Other examples are the European Centre for Social Welfare Policy and Research, already mentioned, Childwatch and the Child Rights Information Network (CRIN).

In Europe, in the field of education on children's rights, we have (since 1991) the Erasmus network, linking 13 universities. In addition to a student exchange scheme, the programme also includes an annual European course on the Rights of the Child. As well as this, the University of Gent has, since 1990, organized an annual postgraduate course on children's rights. Since 1996 this has been supplemented by an international interdisciplinary course.

Also co-ordinated by the university of Gent and with the support of Unesco, in 1996 there was established the *Children's Rights Universities Network* (CRUN).

Crun links 11 universities around the world in regions identified by Unesco. These universities committed themselves to implement the Convention on the Rights of the Child at an academic level, c.q. academic education, research and providing services. The aim is to multiply this strategy to the national as well as to the regional level.

Magazines are important instruments in keeping networks together, offering partners an opportunity for regular contact. Examples of such magazines are scientific publications, such as the "International Journal of children's rights" and "Childhood", but also magazines like "Initiatives Without Borders", follow-up to the Conference "Voice of the Children", held in 1987.

Last but not least, we have the NGO's in het field of children's rights. As a result of the establishment of the Convention on the Rights of the Child there has been a conspicuous amount of activity by a number of non-governmental organizations (NGO's) that work internationally. There was a genuine NGO lobby concerning the Convention (see infra). One of these NGO's is *Defence for Children International* (DCI), which assumes a major position in the international movement for children's rights. This organization currently has agencies in more than 60 countries on every continent.

In various countries, a range of organizations (including DCI agencies) set up coalitions or collectives for children's rights. On an international level, these national groupings (about fifty of them) are coordinated by the *NGO-group for the Convention on the Rights of the Child,* whose headquarters are in Geneva.

The Convention also forms the frame of reference for the operations of UNICEF, the United Nations' Children's Fund. This means that the *National UNICEF Committees,* working as NGO's in 38 countries, also have the task of promoting the implementation of the Convention on the Rights of the Child in their own country. There is still little sign of really systematic international (e.g. European) coordination in this respect. It is worth mentioning *Euronet,* a European children's rights network, which, since 1996, has been lobbying to have children included in the basic treaty of the EU when it comes up for revision. This would give a legislative basis to a European policy on children. A very specific international NGO is the *International Bureau for Children's Rights* which is organising on a regular basis so-called *international tribunals* concerning specific articles of the Convention.

Chapter 3

RECENT TRENDS: CHILD-IMAGE AND THE HUMAN RIGHTS PROJECT

1. Child-image and law

The different elements in the debate on the deconstruction and reconstruction of the child-image, (referred to above), are visible in various respects of children's daily existence.

It is therefore interesting to find out to what extent the same debate, and especially trends towards change, are reflected in current legislation and case law. We chose the law as our field of study, because changes in the law – known for its inertia – reflect broader changes in society as a whole.

We asked ourselves particularly whether the law has contributed to a more positive attitude to children as human beings, and if so to what extent. This is all the more important at the present time because the law is increasingly becoming the (principal) means of obtaining respect.

We asked ourselves this question in the context of two essential elements in the debate: on the one hand, recognition of children as human beings with rights (material rights) of their own, on the other, recognition of their legal capacity (formal rights). Because we were dealing with developments in society as a whole, we also looked beyond the national situation to changes at an international level. For this reason, we also did not limit ourselves to a single part of society (or legal discipline) but will discuss various areas.

It goes without saying that the UN Convention on the Rights of the Child is the most important indicator of change. We will return to the Convention in chapters 4, 6 and 7.

Finally, it is not our ambition to cover everything. A number of striking examples are given, however, mainly because of their heuristic value.

1.1. The child - bearer of (fundamental) rights

1.1.1. *(Draft) rules*

Already in its Recommendation 874 (1974) on "a European Charter on the Rights of the Child" the Council of Europe states: "Children should no longer be considered parents' property, but should be recognised as individuals with their own rights and needs". That children are human beings is also stressed in later Council of Europe recommendation (Recommendation 1121 (1990)) "on the rights of children": "Considering that, along with the right to be protected, children have rights they may independently exercise themselves – even against opposing adults".

The recommendations clearly indicate the direction the debate on children's right to self-determination is taking.

In the Netherlands legalising euthanasia became an issue in the eighties, and special attention was paid to the situation of minors. The authoritative State Committee, which studied the matter, came to the conclusion that an age limit is not desirable for euthanasia. According to the Committee, what counts is not the age of the child, but its understanding of the illness and the implications of its request to terminate its life.

The State Committee agreed with the advice of the equally authoritative National Health Council, which refuses all forms of treatment for minors without their consent, provided the minor disposes of the so called power of discernement.

We find another example in Belgian legislation on Welfare Centres. Article 1 of the law of 8th July 1976 states that: "each individual has the right to be provided with social services ... to ensure (s)he may lead a life of dignity."

Minors have the same rights to be provided with social services and discrimination based on age is excluded. However to get this far, it took a judgement by the Council of State (see below).

The debate has also had noticeable consequences for Family Law. There have been particularly interesting developments concerning the right of children to be heard in divorce cases.

In the Federal Republic of Germany "das Gesetz zur Neuregelung des Rechts der Elterlichen Sorge" (1979) forces magistrates to hear children as of the age of 14. Legislation in the Netherlands (1989) and France (1987) contains similar provisions, as of the age of 12 in the Netherlands and 13 in France. Belgium has had a legislation regulating the right of children to be heard since 1994.

However, strangely enough, there is no legislation in these countries forcing magistrates to take the opinion of a minor into account. There is no sanction if the minor's opinion is ignored. Moreover the child heard cannot appeal against the decision taken. This is why some people feel the only solution to this problem is to recognise the child as an equal party in the litigation.

It goes without saying that the adoption of the Convention on the Rights of the Child was also an important event, reflecting growing consensus on recognition of the child as a full person with his/her own rights (see below).

In this regard the fact that the constitution of a number of States make reference to children's rights is a powerful consequence of the adoption of the Convention on the Rights of the Child and illustrates the growing recognition of children as bearers of rights since then: Belgium (article 22bis), Poland (article 72), Portugal (article 69), Slovenia (article 56), South Africa (article 28).

1.1.2. *Case law*

An analysis of the jurisprudence by the European Court of Human Rights in Strasbourg leads to similar conclusions on recognition of the child as a person with his/her own (human) rights.

In the Bouamar ruling (29th February 1988) the court found the Belgian State guilty of unlawful imprisonment of minors by juvenile courts. The ruling refers to article 5, § 4 of the European Convention on the protection of Human rights (ECHR), which says: "Everyone who is deprived of his liberty by arrest or detention shall be entitled to take proceedings by which the lawfulness of his detention shall be decided speedily by a court and his release ordered if the detention is not lawful".

In other words, the right of the person arrested or detained, even if he is under age, to have the legality of his detention tested by court had been infringed.

This is not the only case in which the European Court has recognised the human rights of minors. Already in the years between 1984 and 1991 the European Court dealt with no less than 19 cases involving minors.

The Warwick case is another example. This case, which was dealt with by former the European Commission of Human Rights, was a complaint made by a girl under the age of majority about corporal punishment she had received in her school, which she had felt to be humiliating and an infringement of article 3 of the ECHR: "No one shall be subjected to torture or to inhuman or degrading treatment or punishment".

In the course of the procedure, the British government was urged by the European Commission to introduce legislation banning corporal punishment in schools. This legislation has now been issued.

This evolution which started in the eighties is continuing unabated today. Many more examples can be given. They are even the subject of separate research.

The debate on children's competence is inextricably linked to their recognition as people with their own rights. Or to put it in other words, are children capable of exercising their rights independently?

1.2. Children's legal capacity

In most countries in the West, being underage is synonymous with being legally incapable. In other words, even if, in principle, minors are regarded as persons with their own rights, in practice, they are considered incapable of exercising these rights. The rights of minors have to be exercised by those who have parental authority. Legally speaking, parental authority and minority are therefore complementary concepts. However, this situation often puts obstacles in the way of (re)value children's position in society. As an illustration, we quote from the opinion of the Belgian Council of State, Legislation section, on the law extending compulsory education (1983).

The original bill stated: "Every young person is entitled to basic education for a period of 12 consecutive years, starting in the school year which begins during the calendar year in which the young person becomes 6, this to contribute, on the one hand, to his education in the personal, family and social spheres, and on the other, to a suitable preparation for professional life. Consequently parents or those in authority over young people have to ensure the young person ...".

On this passage, the Council of State made the following remark: "This text is complicated because it describes the right to basic education as a right of the young person, while civil law rules on legal capacity and the definition of compulsory education clearly indicate that said right can only be claimed by and against the parents or those who have parental authority. In other words, the person who has to exercise the right is also the person against whom any complaint of failure to exercise the rights must be brought. To avoid this, for reasons of simplicity and with a view to improving the structure of the text, it seems desirable to limit the definition of compulsory education to a definition of the obligations it entails (...).

The fact that there are changes in the definition of legal (in)capacity is shown by two rulings handed down by Belgium's highest administrative court: the Council of State. We will quote extensively from the first ruling, concerning access to Municipal Welfare Centres, because it is a perfect illustration of this development.

In ruling 30.895 of 7th October 1988, the Council states:

"*Having regard to* article 1 of the law of 8th July 1976 recognising the right of *each individual* to be provided with social services, to ensure (s)he may lead a life of dignity.;
having regard to article 57 of the same law, which gives Municipal Welfare Centres the task of providing social services to persons and families;
having regard to article 71, which states in its first paragraph, that *each individual* has the right of appeal against a decision on the provision of social services which concerns him (...);
Considering that from all these provisions it can be deduced that the right to receive social services can be exercised by all individuals who are destitute and therefore not in a position to lead a life of dignity;
that a minor who, rightly or wrongly, has left the home of his parents and is destitute, is also *personally entitled* to this right;
that, although in principle this right is exercised by the legal representatives of the minor on his/her behalf, *the minor's legal capacity has to be recognised for him/her to be able to exercise his/her right to social services independently, if his legal representatives do not exercise it on his/her behalf*".

We find the same rationale in a later decision (22nd February 1989) by the same administrative court, which declared admissible a complaint by a minor, concerning his irrevocable expulsion from a secondary school. In fact, this decision went even further, doing away with the condition that the minor's legal representatives must have refused to act on his behalf.

The former European Commission and Court of Human Rights also seems to have come out in favour of a new approach to the principle of legal incapacity. Article 25 of the ECHR establishes an individual right to complain, both for adults and children. Minors are therefore regarded as capable of taking a case to the European Court. Thus the Commission declared admissible a complaint by a 14 year old girl, who had been forced to return home, after having "been away" for a few days with her boyfriend (Application No. 6753/74, X. and Y. v. the Netherlands). Article 6 of the ECHR confers the right to a fair trial to everyone.

According to the Court, those who are legally incapable (i.e. minors) must also have access to the Court. On the basis of article 13 of the ECHR, minors who according to their national legislation do not have access to the court, can lodge a complaint about this with the European Court.

Although the competence debate remains largely theoretical, it can be said that the ECHR has strengthened children's legal position and increased their legal capacity.

In Belgium, in the meantime, more and more Courts regard claims by minors for financial support as admissible. The following statement by the Mons Justice of the Peace (19th April 1989) is quoted as a remarkable example: "... that the legal incapacity of the minor should be regarded as a means of protecting him/her, rather than as a penalty imposed on him/her; that the fact of the plaintiff's bringing the case should not in any sense be held against him/her, it should indeed be regarded as evidence of his/her maturity."

We find a similar rationale in a ruling by the Amsterdam Court (13th July 1989). A complaint by a girl under the age of majority was declared admissible on the grounds that her (subjective) right to freedom and safety, the protection of which is guaranteed for all persons, had been infringed by her father. The court did not invoke the girl's legal incapacity, because it considered her capable of discernment and therefore able to make an independent judgement on the best course of action.

In fact more and more national as well as international jurisprudence subscribes to the "pragmatic trend" discussed in chapter 2.

1.3. Conclusion

This brief excursion into the field of law, and more particularly, into the field of (draft) legislation and case law, demonstrates the fact that attitudes to children (child-images) have been evolving over the last few decades. We have focused on two fundamental issues in the debate: the child as a bearer of rights (not only preferential rights for children, but also fundamental human rights), and as a person capable of exercising these rights independently. Legal incapacity remains the rule (in the case of minors' subjective rights), but more and more often the competence of minors is recognised. There appears to be growing respect for children.

And yet, one can only wonder whether this evolution in the law is not merely reflection of changes which have already occurred in society as a whole, rather than leading the way; in other words legislation is re-active rather than pro-active.

Would it not be preferable for the law to play a more active role in promoting change and greater humanity and respect in our relationship with children? There are indications this may happen. In the field of human rights there is a similar shift towards a more pro-active approach in law.

Law without counter borders. Indeed quite a lot of problems encountered by people, and therefore also by children, have their roots at a macro-social level. Much effort therefore goes into producing (human rights) instruments to generate change at that level.

The UN Convention on the Rights of the Child is such an instrument. This is witnessed by the fact that since the Convention on the Rights of the Child has come into force, *emancipatory* jurisprudence and regulations have nearly always been influenced by this Convention. Before we go into the Convention, we will consider the second trend of recent years: the human rights project.

2. The human rights project

In the autumn of 1988, the West watched in amazement as in the Eastern Bloc one satellite state after another regained its freedom. Everything took place at lightning speed, and seemingly effortlessly. Before these developments would have been regarded as impossible. None of the revolutions in the East could have happened without the relentless effort of human rights organisations. Dissidents, Neues Forum, Citizen's Forum, Charter 77, Helsinki Committees, ..., were the bedrock on which the repressed peoples of these countries founded their hopes of liberation. In other words, these far-reaching changes were largely the result of a human rights project, frequently regarded as no more than an abstract concept, yet always there, and particularly influential in the second half of the twentieth century.

Let us now discuss a number of aspects of this trend, i.e. increasing attention for human rights in society as a whole.

2.1. Historical background

Respect for human beings is a long-established tenet of most cultures. Protecting the defenceless was usually a matter for the gods or their representatives, i.e. the rulers. To the Greeks, man was the measure of all things. The Romans developed a legal system, the main principle of which was that all "free" citizens (i.e. not slaves) were equal. The

Judaeo-Christian tradition was based on brotherly love and tolerance (the Ten Commandments).

However a look at the history of the West reveals that large-scale repression was in fact the rule. The development of the churches and its paradoxical intertwining with the state created a strong powerbase, power structures (the absolute rulers) and an accompanying repression, based on lineage, social class and rank.

The voyages of discovery revealed violations of the most elementary rights of other peoples and civilisations. In other words, although lip-service has always been paid to respect for human beings, in actual fact things were quite different.

2.1.1. *Historical milestones*

Our present views on human rights stem from the influence of the age of Reason, and the Enlightenment. It is understandable we know very little of institutionalised respect for human beings before that. And yet the first human rights instrument is often considered to have been the *Magna Carta* (1215). The English nobility negotiated granting of a number of rights by Prince John in exchange for allowing his accession to the throne. Among other things, the Magna Carta bans imprisonment without trial.

Later on, in 1689, it was once again the English nobility which laid the foundation for the first constitutional monarchy with the *Bill of Rights*. The Bill of Rights curtailed the king's absolute power introducing of a number of constitutional rights and freedoms. A major share of power now lay in the hands of Parliament (the House of Lords and the House of Commons).

The American Revolution (against the English) led to the *Declaration of Independence*, adopted on 4th July 1776, containing the same provisions as the Bill of Rights. The basic principles, enshrined in the Declaration by Thomas Jefferson, were that all men are created equal and have the right to life, liberty and the pursuit of happiness. Jefferson did not however succeed in abolishing slavery, which only disappeared in 1863 after the American Civil War.

Subsequently, the ideas and achievements of the American Revolution influenced the *French Revolution* (14th July 1789). The *Declaration of Human Rights and Civil Rights* was drawn up. Although the rights it established (among others, the right to life and to own property, freedom of opinion, of the press, and of association, ...) were mainly enjoyed by the *bourgeoisie* (Karl Marx would refer to these as the rights of the selfish), they became a model for a number of constitutions in Europe and South America. Many of these rights were later included in the Universal Declaration of Human Rights (1948).

The rights established were the so-called traditional fundamental rights: political rights and civil rights (the first generation of human rights). However because of Karl Marx's criticism of what he bourgeois rights ("not everybody is equal", "what is the point in being free, if it remains impossible to lead a life worthy of man") and the beginning of the struggle for emancipation, more and more attention was focused on social rights (i.e. the second generation).

These were enshrined for the very first time in the *Declaration of the rights of the exploited working class* during the *Russian Revolution* (1917). Subsequently, economic, social and cultural rights were included in Russia's socialist constitution (1918), which established the right to work, education, housing, medical care, ... and the state's duty to contribute to the well-being of society.

Although the ideas of the Enlightenment (e.g. sovereignty in the hands of the people, rather than of the king) became known internationally, and some individuals (Jefferson, La Fayette, Marx, ...) succeeded in exporting the concept of human rights to other countries, human rights remained mainly a matter for national concern until the first half of 20th century. It is however important that what were originally only moral codes (declarations) became rules conferring positive entitlements, by, e.g. their inclusion in a national constitution, and thus acquiring the force of law.

2.1.1. *Internationalisation*

The first Geneva Convention (1864), promoted by the Red Cross, and subsequently the The Hague Convention (1899), both dealing with humanitarian rights in situations of war, constituted the first steps towards the establishment of human rights valid beyond single states. Not until after the First World War, however, did this internationalisation began to take place; international community started to organise itself and created institutions.

Indeed in 1919 the *League of Nations* was set up to maintain world peace. Its members are states. In 1926 the League succeeded in adopting the International Convention on the Abolition of Slavery. It failed however in its main objective, which was to prevent the Second World War.

In 1945, immediately after the Second World War the United Nations Organisation (UN) was set up. Its aim was to maintain international peace and security, and to promote international co-operation in economic, social, cultural and humanitarian matters.

The UN Charter repeatedly refers to respect for human rights and fundamental freedoms, which are regarded as the very foundation of peace and democracy. It is clear that the international community wishes to avoid a repetition of the barbarities of the Second World War. At the time the international community consisted mainly of some fifty countries in the West. After the period of decolonisation at the end of the Fifties, more and more states from other parts of the world acceded. On 31 December 1999 the UN had 188 member states.

Barely 3 years later, on 10th December 1948, the *Universal Declaration of Human Rights* is adopted by the UN General Assembly almost unanimously, with no votes against and 8 abstentions from among others the communist countries, Saudi Arabia and South Africa.

The Universal Declaration obviously attaches a good deal of importance to traditional human rights (political rights and civil rights), but also, significantly, deals with economic, social and cultural rights.

As already stated, a *Declaration* is a significant moral code, but it is not law. The transition from the Declaration to binding rules will take quite a while. The *International Covenant on Economic, Social and Cultural Rights* and the *International Covenant on Civil and Political Rights* were adopted only in 1966. Together, the Declaration (1948) and the two International Covenants (1966) are called the *International Bill of Human Rights.* They must be considered as the greatest and most important human rights instruments.

2.1.3. *Rapid increase in the number of human rights instruments, regionalisation and binding effect*

After the 1948 Universal Declaration the number of human rights instruments increases extremely rapidly.

While the following list is by no means complete, it is impressive all the same:

- 1948: Universal Declaration of Human Rights
- 1950: European Convention on the Protection of Human rights and Fundamental Freedoms (/Protocols)
- 1951: Convention relating to the Status of Refugees (Protocol relating to the Status of Refugees - 1967)
- 1952: Convention on the Political Rights of Women
- 1954: Convention relating to the Status of Stateless Persons
- 1959: Declaration on the Rights of the Child

- 1961: European Social Charter (revised in 1996)
- 1965: International Convention on the Elimination of All Forms of Racial Discrimination
- 1966: International Covenant on Civil and Political Rights
- 1966: International Covenant on Economic, Social and Cultural Rights
- 1969: American Convention on Human Rights
- 1970: Declaration on the Rights of Mentally Retarded Persons
- 1973: International Convention on the Suppression and Punishment of the Crime of Apartheid
- 1975: Final Act, Helsinki (Conference on Security and Co-operation in Europe)
- 1976: Convention on the Elimination of All Forms of Discrimination against Women
- 1981: African Charter on Human and Peoples' Rights
- 1983: Universal Islamic Declaration of Human Rights (The League of Arab States)
- 1985: Declaration of Basic Principles of Justice for Victims of Crime and Abuse of Power
- 1985: United Nations Minimum Rules for the Administration of Juvenile Justice ("The Bejing Rules")
- 1987: Recommendation R(87)21 on the Assistance to Victims and Prevention of Victimisation
- 1989: Convention on the Rights of the Child
- 1990: African Charter on the Rights and Welfare of the Child.
- 1992: Resolution of the European Parliament on a European Charter of the Rights of the Child
- 1992: Declaration of Rio on Environment and Development (Agenda 21)
- 1996: European Convention on the Exercise of Children's Rights
- 2000: Optional protocol to the Convention on the Rights of the Child on the sale of children, child prostitution and child pornography;
- 2000: Optional protocol to the Convention on the Rights of the Child on involvement of children in armed conflicts.

Besides these UN and regional instruments, the Conference on Private International Law in The Hague very recently adopted the following conventions: *Convention on the Civil Aspects of International Child Abduction* (1980), *Convention on Protection of Children and Co-operation in Respect of Intercountry Adoption* (1993), and the *Convention on jurisdiction, Applicable Law, Recognition, Enforcement and Co-operation in respect of Parental Responsibility and Measures for the Protection of Children* (1996).

An impressive list indeed. As of now there are apparently more than 80 international and regional treaties on human rights. There is a fundamental difference between declarations of intent, which are not binding, and treaties, which are. The above list refers both to *declarations of intent* and to *treaties*. Not only the number of texts is important or even the transition from moral code (declaration) to legally binding rules (convention/treaty), but especially the extent to which the areas covered by such rights has expanded.

It is also striking that, since 1948, more and more declarations and treaties have been adopted which concern on the one hand *specific groups* (children, women, refugees, the stateless, workers, ...) and on the other *specific problems* (genocide, war crimes, torture, racial discrimination, ...).

Besides universal instruments there are also *regional human rights instruments*. They are adopted by and on behalf of extensive areas (Europe, Africa, America) where there is, theoretically at least, a greater degree of cultural identity. In fact, the ambition of achieving universal human rights, assuming this to be possible, often leads to vague and imprecise wording (in order to achieve a consensus), making it difficult to turn these rights into positive rules, precisely defined (for the purposes of the law). This is why certain states, with cultural affinities, prefer regional treaties.

We have, for instance, the *European* Convention on Human Rights (1950), covering the 41 Council of Europe members, the *American* Convention on Human Rights (1969), ratified only by Central and South American countries, and the *African* Charter on Human Rights and the Rights of Peoples (1981).

Rapid translation of *declarations* into *legally binding treaties* (sometimes called "hard law") is also extremely important. This provides the moral intention with a legal basis for taking action.

The first far-reaching international treaty was adopted as early as November 4th 1950 in Rome: the "European Convention on the Protection of Human Rights and Fundamental Freedoms" (the ECHR for short). It entered into force on September 3rd 1953. All 41 member states of the Council of Europe have signed and ratified it.

The ECHR deals mainly with the political rights and civil rights contained in the Universal Declaration. Implementation of the ECHR is monitored by the European Court of Human Rights, in Strasbourg. Proceedings can only be instituted at the European Court provided alternatives offered by national legal systems have been exhausted.

The Court's rulings are binding on member states. In this sense the ECHR is the very first binding international human rights instrument.

Besides the ECHR and the European Social Charter, in this context we also have to mention the extremely important treaties adopted by the UN in 1966: the International Covenant on Economic, Social and Cultural Rights (now ratified by 142 countries) and the Covenant on Civil and Political Rights (144 ratifications).

This last treaty is complemented by two optional protocols one on individual complaints (now ratified by 94 countries) and another on the interstate complaints (43 ratifications). The UN Committee on Human Rights is in charge of international monitoring of this treaty. The Committee is made up of 18 independent experts, who deal with reports submitted by states on steps taken to implement the treaty, and with notification of infringements under the terms of the Optional Protocols.

The International Covenant on Economic, Social and Cultural Rights is monitored by the 18 members of the Committee on Economic, Social and Cultural Rights.

These Covenants round off translation of the content of the Universal Declaration into legally binding rules. They can therefore be considered the most important human rights instruments.

Although in principle the ECHR and the UN Covenants should also apply to children (and practical application of the Covenants to children has only just begun), in 1989 the international community decided to draw up a separate Convention on the Rights of the Child to be approved and ratified by the member states of the UN. Again a legally binding instrument. We will return to the Convention in more detail in another chapter.

2.1.4. *Third generation* of human rights

Although in principle all human rights are interconnected and there is no question of precedence, historically speaking there have been three generations of human rights.

The *first generation* goes all the way back to the 18th century. We are thinking here mainly of the Declaration of the Rights of Man and of the Citizen (1789), which contained *traditional civil and political rights*, such as the right to freedom of opinion, freedom of the press, the right of assembly, the right to life, etc.. They could be described as the first defensive weapons against sovereign rulers. However important a first step these rights were, all the state had to do (to respect these liberal freedoms) was remain aloof, and refrain from doing certain things it had done before.

The *second generation* of human rights displays a far more offensive attitude to the state. Abstention from exaggerated interference (first generation) is now complemented by an urgent appeal to a sense of social responsibility on the part of the state. Recognising *economic, social and cultural human rights* (right to a minimum income, work, health care, education, leisure, ...) means the state has to act. The second generation, dealing in essence with *social justice,* was enshrined in legally binding texts for the first time in the Russian Constitution (1918).

In the last few years, there has been more and more talk of *peoples' rights,* a third generation of human rights. Here we are dealing with so-called *solidarity rights,* such as the right to peace, a healthy environment, cultural integrity, self-government, etc. (A rough estimate is that there are more than 3,500 peoples or ethnic groups in the world which are distinct from other analogous groups.) Debate about the actual shape and content of these new rights is still going on. For instance, in the summer of 1992, under the auspices of the UN, a world conference on the environment and development (UNCED) took place in Rio and led to the adoption by 179 states of Agenda 21. The concept of *sustainable development* which is developing from this could well become the basis for both generations of human rights. The action programme *Agenda 21* adopted at the conference shows that the Declaration of Rio is already starting to be implemented in spite of the fact that is has no legally binding value.

2.2. The shift from an instrumental function to a function of legal protection

2.1.1. *Social control and the instrumental function of laws and welfare provision*

(Criminal) law and law enforcement are traditionally instrumental in character. They are a means, an instrument, used by the authorities to guide society in the right direction. The 'right direction', indeed, because under the influence of the ideas of the age of Reason and the Enlightenment, in the minds of Western man there is (still) an overwhelming consensus on what society should be like and how it ought to evolve. Harmony, perfect happiness, absence of suffering, ... are fundamental components of this prospective utopia.

Central to the debate is how human beings by their actions can achieve the one and avoid the other. In the forefront of this philosophy is the idea that man is a rational being not dependent on destiny or divine planning (as in the Middle Ages), but autonomous. At the very most, man is considered to be temporarily dependent on the laws of nature. Temporarily, because increasing knowledge of these laws (which in principle can be acquired), will enable man to control nature, and, by removing obstacles and using all available means, to achieve our (future) happy society.

It is undeniable that in the physical world there have been some pretty fair achievements.

By analogy with our knowledge of, and intervention in nature, we also attempt to understand and plan human society. From the very beginning of the age of Reason and the Enlightenment all sorts of instruments have been designed to this end. We have, for instance, the Utopian desire of the enlightened criminal lawyers (e.g. Beccaria, et al.) to create a crime-free society, by underpinning criminal law with such principles as legality, equality, proportionality, due process... founded on the Cartesian image of man (rationality, free will, moral responsibility, ...). Enlightened criminal lawyers believe fighting crime is less important than preventing crime, because man, being rational, constantly weighs pros and cons. Through the criminal law, man gains insights into what is and is not allowed, he knows the possible cons (punishments), and as a rational being he will be able to make a conscious choice (free will) to do good and abstain from doing evil (crime). If he chooses to do evil, he is personally and fully responsible for his actions (moral responsibility). Fighting crime (the exception rather than the rule) would become more humane because less arbitrary and not conducted out of desire for revenge (an eye for an eye). In other words, traditional criminal law is an illustration of belief in the possibility of designing instruments (feasibility) to create a (future) enlightened society, which would also be free of crime. Creating a new society is considered even more important than removing obstacles. Criminal law, the administration of justice, law enforcement and ... fighting crime become mainly instrumental.

The fact that that which is undesirable (crime), continues to occur, is a social problem in this approach, because it constitutes an obstacle to fulfilling the dream of a crime-free society. The phenomenon is however considered to be of a temporary nature, which will soon (in the future) be removed by extending our knowledge of the rules (causes) governing it. As soon as we know the causes, we stop (only) punishing criminals, but we can remove the causes (be they individual or social), correct them or prevent them from happening (prevention).

In other words, social problems are situations which are regarded as obstacles to the creation of an enlightened society. They are solved by correcting deviations on the basis of accurate knowledge of their causes. Sociology, in general, and criminology, in particular, are (still) the expression of our hopeful and frantic search for knowledge of causes. The search itself (almost as if it were in the nature of things) proceeds along the same path as research in the natural sciences, following the lines of physics and medicine. One of the main characteristics of this search is linear causality: causal factors are regarded as direct causes of the phenomenon. Causes are looked for 'inside' the individual, considered as possessing certain characteristics which cause the problem (intra-psychic view). The phenomenon is isolated from its context and studied as a technical problem in which there are no values at stake, in the hope that by doing this a catalogue of causal factors can be established which can be regarded as responsible for social problems.

People who are considered to be potential risks have to be located at an early stage; even before they can become a hindrance, ... in fact before they commit crimes. Crime prevention is considered even more important than tracking down criminals. Social sciences play their part in preserving law and order, by helping to locate and treat of problem cases (correction and avoidance of recidivism) but also help to promote the idea of prevention.

Increased knowledge, especially of the laws of nature, also meant increased desire to apply knowledge (technology). This inevitably led to a technological explosion and finally to the industrial revolution and its social consequences: massive migration to industrial centres, neglect of children caused by the long hours and exhausting working conditions of their parents, use of children as cheap and amenable labour, bad housing, etc. These "new" social problems were considered dangerous and an obstacle to progress towards enlightened society. The church and philanthropists were the first to attack these obstacles by alleviating the worst suffering. They did not do this without self-interest, because there were conditions attached to the help given. In exchange those who were helped were expected to accept middle class norms. Welfare, as a social phenomenon, turns into a moral crusade, extending social control over workers and undermining the incipient social struggle.

A good example is the child-protection movement, which gained international importance around the same time. It was felt there was a risk that the circumstances in which children were brought up could predispose them to deviant behaviour and juvenile delinquency (neglect = predelinquency, see A. Aichorn). This risk was the direct cause of a radical change in civil law, allowing the option to remove children from parental authority. Loss of parental authority was no longer considered an additional punishment for having committed a crime. It became a civil sanction, a change in the relationship between parents and children to prevent neglect. This is an example of how a social problem (neglect of children because of atrocious living conditions) was turned into an educational problem (parents deemed incapable of bringing up their children) and how intervention by the state, on the authority of a judge came to be considered acceptable. Or of how welfare (through the courts) becomes social control. The picture is all too clear.

In criminal law there is a similar development. First – this was already the case in the Napoleonic Code – it was accepted that minors who had committed a crime without being aware of the gravity of their actions (and would therefore be acquitted) could be held at Her Majesty's pleasure, which meant they could be locked up in an institution. The rationale was that a child who, at such a tender age, was already capable of such actions might well become chronically delinquent and therefore needed re-education.

The child protection laws, adopted at the beginning of the twentieth century in Europe, such as the Belgian Law of 1912, followed the same principle and indeed went even further. For instance in Belgium, children, for whom 'educational measures' are considered more appropriate, are dealt with entirely outside the criminal law. However this Belgian law not only covers juvenile delinquents, but also those who might become delinquent. In article 15, the law literally states that minors "who undertake activities which might lead to crime" can be dealt with by the courts: i.e. predelinquency. In doing this, the Belgian law relinquishes traditional criminal law principles (legality, equality, proportionality, etc.). Moreover, these early (preventive) interventions are depicted as being in the best interests of the minor: i.e. welfare. Obviously we are in fact not talking about the best interests of the child but progress to an enlightened society: i.e. social control. This is evident, because if we had the best interests of predelinquent children and their neglected families at heart, we would by now have given proper thought to a genuine welfare structure. In other words, a more active and far-reaching social policy would have been implemented. But in fact welfare is always forced upon people, through the courts, at as early a stage as possible. This is called a crime-premium approach. This approach is not only used with problem families, but also in other cases of social problems (poverty, mendacity, etc.).

As the first half of the twentieth century progresses, more and more often social control is exerted using knowledge acquired in the behavioural sciences: psychiatry, psychology, sociology, criminology, medicine, ... Charitable institutions, traditionally run by volunteers, are gradually taken over by professionals. The objective, however, remains the same: social control. This is illustrated by the fact that the first Belgian schools for social work (1920) were set up not by the Education Minister, but by the Minister of Justice. Wherever there is formal, and later on also less formal, social control, so-called social services pop up (child protection agencies, probation services, ...). The link is clear. Welfare and formal social control are both part of the instrumental function of criminal law and the administration of justice.
The main, in fact only, achievement of the welfare system is that under its influence social control has become more humane. Steps are always taken because of deviation from what is considered socially desirable and the objective is always redirection towards that which is considered socially desirable. Forms of welfare which want to go further, may be well-intentioned and may have some effect, but are mistaken as to the main objective to be achieved. This objective is clear.

Friction, discussion, ... cannot be avoided and at some point in time will reach a peak of intensity. Let us examine why.

2.2.2. *Law enforcement and welfare in defence of rights and emancipation*

We have already demonstrated that for a long time there was a strong, dominant consensus on what was considered socially desirable and also on *how* (using which instruments) the desired society could be brought into being. Obviously there was also agreement on what was considered undesirable and *how* (using which instruments) that which was undesirable was resisted and prevented. Criminal law and the administration of justice, with the help of first charitable initiatives, originally pursuing social objectives, later on of professional welfare structures, were good examples of the unity of purpose in designing the instruments required.

The prerequisite for this system to function is broad consensus on social reality and, more particularly, on what is deemed desirable. It is still functioning today. In the twentieth century (especially the second half), the identity and strength (dominance) of consensus began to be eroded. In a number of areas, it became clear the Utopian (i.e. crime-free) society, with everything needed to achieve it, was generating many harmful side-effects (repression, alienation, destruction of the environment, etc.). Consensus was becoming shaky, even on what was to be regarded as deviance (see radical criminology, labelling theory, ...). But there were also problems with existing forms of law enforcement, some of them indeed caused by welfare structures. There was growing doubt about a system which made crime a purely legal phenomenon, and excluded the individual citizen (whether criminal or victim) from any meaningful role in the process of criminal law. It became more and more striking that only facts which were regarded as 'functional' in view of the 'charge' were perceived to be 'relevant' and that all other facts were dismissed as 'irrelevant'. Characteristics were attributed to citizens, and others taken from them to suit a procedure in which they played no part. Because this control system began to be regarded as alienating, quite early on steps were taken to humanise it. Recent attention to the legal position of the perpetrator is part of this effort (as is yet more recent attention to the legal position of the victim).

However these developments are mainly taking place within the system of social control we have just described. It has little to do with real emancipation and meeting citizens' needs. In other words, although there have been technical improvements in the methods used, welfare itself has not yet changed fundamentally.

And yet these improvements were only possible because of a number of other more far-reaching changes in society. These changes can be regarded as a reaction to the harmful side-effects of enlightened society. The Second World War was an important (for our subject perhaps even dramatic) turning point.

After the crisis years of the Thirties, and gloom caused by the war, more and more people began to doubt the consensus society. In this development, a fundamental part was played by the increasing international importance (in society as a whole) of ideas on *human rights*, which multiplied rapidly (see dates), and were reinforced in their content and status (treaties instead of declarations). Based at first on moral authority (Universal Declaration of Human Rights), human rights then became legally binding, and positive law (European Convention on Human Rights).

The law, which previously was limited to a purely *instrumental function*, began to change. Its *legal protective* function became more and more dominant. Officers of the law (e.g. the police) therefore acquire a new, fundamental task in addition to the one they already held ... though the two were virtually indistinguishable. In cases of rape, for instance, the victim no longer merely 'serves' as evidence of a crime (instrumental function), rather the victim is now perceived to have enforceable rights too, which not only deserve respect, but must also be enforced in practice (protective function).

The number of international declarations and conventions has increased substantially since 1948 (see above). This has had more effect on welfare and social policy than is generally assumed. We have already said that the extension of traditional fundamental rights (political rights of freedom and equality) to 'social' fundamental rights was an important development. It was in fact discovered that the influence of the American and French revolutions had led to traditional human rights (thanks to J. Locke and other enlightened philosophers) becoming part of many national cultures in the 19th century, these political rights had little meaning if it remained economically impossible for people to lead a life of dignity. The first reference to fundamental social rights in positive law appeared in Russia in the "Declaration of the rights of the exploited working class" (1918) and in the Russian Constitution.

It would take until after the Second World War before this right to a decent existence, enshrined in economic, social and cultural rights, was recognised internationally. There was the European Social Charter in 1961 and in 1966 the UN adopted the International Covenant on Economic, Social and Cultural Rights. Through these international conventions these ideas gradually took root at national level. Things began to happen. Belgian Legislation establishing the Right to Subsistence Income, adopted on August 1st 1974, is a good example of this second generation of human rights. Besides the *right to* financial support, the *right to* access to welfare in general was established in the "Law on Public Welfare Centres" adopted on July 8th 1976. Article 1 states literally: "*Every* person is entitled to be provided with social services, to allow *everyone* to lead a life *worthy of a human being*. Public welfare centres were set up to provide these services, under the conditions laid down by law".

The right to financial support and to welfare became enforceable through court rulings in industrial disputes, even in appeal cases.

While there are many, well-founded complaints about the application of national legislation, there is no doubt that by enshrining the right to welfare in binding rules, in positive law, an attempt is made to bring about a radical change in society. However, social fundamental rights were not included in the Belgian Constitution (article 23) until 1994.

In the welfare sector a similar development is taking place: here the (human) rights approach, described above, is labelled 'emancipation'. This concept was originally introduced in the so-called 'alternative' sector, 'alternative' to be understood as indicating a newly-developed, broader view on human rights (legal protection), including a refusal to contribute to social control (the instrumental function mentioned above). In this way, the welfare sector tried to keep its distance from the social control function in which it had traditionally been involved. That this was an entirely new approach was not clear at the outset and its significance has still not been fully grasped. There were, however, fierce discussions between advocates of the two views which did clarify matters to a certain extent. Child-protection is a good example. Debate on the contradiction between welfare and the legal approach was carried out against the background of ideas on deviant behaviour. Welfare (the best interests of the child) is regarded as a form of social control, exerted mainly on children/families belonging to lower social classes. Thus child-protection is regarded as a 'political' instrument used to preserve the existing social and economic order, that is, as an instrument for enforcing discipline.

Welfare, in this view, should not be based on formal stipulations (the legal approach) but on the client's subjective needs (rights). Its aim is to mobilise its forces, limit its dependence and increase its freedom of action. The objective is to emancipate and to build a horizontal, rather than vertical, relationship between client and welfare structures, a relationship based on trust.

This has become clearer only later through the children's rights movement, which started focusing, within the concept of emancipation, on the material rights aspect (see chapter 2). Apart from a contribution to humanising social control, mentioned above, and increased focus on legal situation, at first not much was achieved. Other than stimulating debate on changes in society, leading ultimately to binding rights to welfare (without social control), indicating changing ideas in society on what is socially desirable and on what constitutes a social problem.

Which brings us back to our starting point: our view of social problems. It will be clear to everyone that because of the growing importance of the human rights perspective, new definitions of those people involved are worked out, and of those who used to be considered problem cases (target groups such as young people, women, migrants, vagrants, the poor, ...).

In child protection circles claims are made with increasing insistence that it is better to 'support' subproletarian families in formulating strategies for bringing up their children (social policy, right to welfare), rather than take away their educational responsibility by placing their children in institutions in cases of presumed neglect.

There is no doubt – in fact there are more and more examples supporting this point of view – that the change in attitudes to what is socially desirable and to social problems will lead to doubts about the dominant consensus. Increased attention to human rights will play a fundamental part in this process. What this means for law enforcement and welfare can and must be clarified.

2.2.3. *The three strands to the debate*

It is possible to shed some light on the on-going debate on welfare and coercion by paying sufficient attention to the (relatively recent) human rights point of view (shift from object to subject). The following three strands are central to the debate:

a) If the point of departure is the instrumental function, welfare and coercion share largely the same objectives: control, correction and conformity.
b) There is considerable contrast between the frame of reference of the instrumental function (social control) and that of the function of legal protection (emancipation). At the most, they influence one another when attempts are made to humanise control and to improve on legal status.
c) From the point of view of legal protection, parallel objectives and task convergence (or even identity) are possible.

Using these three strands, each reflecting a different attitude to children, it should be possible to analyse properly or even shed different light both on the debate on (new) legislation (e.g. the Convention on the rights of the child) and on the tasks of existing institutions for children, a process which may in the end lead to new rules.

At the moment there is considerable confusion in our relationship with children, because trends affecting the whole of society are slowly producing far-reaching changes. Before we start experimenting at random, it would be best to conduct research and consultation exercises and to inform (both via education and further training) of the changes which are occurring. There are a number of points of interest with regard to legal protection which can be of help in this. We will discuss these below.

2.2.4. Requirements for legal protection

Especially since the Convention on the Rights of the Child has come into force, legal protection has now become an extremely important task with regard to children too. The mere protection of children has evolved into the protection of legally established children's rights. In other words, children are no longer considered as legal objects, but increasingly as legal subjects, bearers of rights.

However, legal protection involves more than drawing up and applying judicial and administrative procedures. A number of simple but essential quality requirements must be fulfilled simultaneously.

1. You have to *have* rights, in other words, the child must be recognised as the bearer of rights.
2. You have to be able to *exercise* these rights. With respect to children, this requirement brings us straight to the debate on competence.
3. If necessary, you have to be able to *enforce* your rights. This is inextricably bound up with the two previous requirements. But this also involves a number of special requirements: the necessity of sufficient and comprehensive legal aid and of sufficient and comprehensive training for magistrates, lawyers, police and all those who are involved with law and the court.
   In the debate on the technical legal aspects, this leads to discussions on the legal capacity of minors, their capacity to act, and more specifically, the right to be heard.
4. You have to be *informed* of your rights, i.e. know your rights. Education on human rights and children's rights in the sense of strengthening mutual respect is sometimes pointed to as one of the most elementary conditions for an effective legal protection.
5. You have to be able to (have someone) defend your *interests*. In view of the weak position of children in the decision-making processes too, representation of interests is extremely important. I have already stressed this importance extensively in chapter 2.

Finally, it should be emphasised again that these quality requirements are inseparable. If either one of them is realised only partially or not at all, then an effective legal protection is seriously threatened.

2.3. Conclusion

The main trends to be observed in the human rights project are:

1. from national to international (regional, universal);
2. from an instrumental function to a legal protection function;
3. from a defensive (re-active) to an offensive (pro-active) approach;

4. towards the production in quick succession (see dates) of numerous texts (see number);
5. from moral obligation (declaration) to legally binding texts (conventions);
6. towards tackling specific problems (torture, racial discrimination, ...) and specific groups (women, children, refugees, ...);
7. towards extending substantive content: fundamental traditional rights, followed by fundamental social rights, and finally rights of peoples (i.e. the three generations).

It is clear that these trends in society, which make up the human rights project and which may be stronger that we suspect even now, will have rapid and far-reaching consequences for our social order.

Chapter 4

UN CONVENTION ON THE RIGHTS OF THE CHILD

The previous chapter dealt with the changes in society which form the backdrop to the UN Convention on the Rights of the Child. In fact, in the last few decades there has been growing support for giving children a fully-fledged position in society. Moreover the concept of *human rights* was introduced in the debate surrounding this issue: "Children are human beings, therefore they are entitled to all human rights."

However the debate on their (legal) competence to exercise these rights independently is not yet over and questions often are raised as to the usefulness and/or necessity of a separate convention on the rights of the child.

The consequence of all this is that today, on account of the processes of deconstruction and reconstruction, we find ourselves in a rather confused situation of transition. On the one hand our old child-image is as forceful and dominant as ever, while on the other children are regarded as entitled to human rights.

It is therefore not surprising that in the Convention on the Rights of the Child, adopted in 1989, we find both child-images. The reader will notice how this essential question (do human rights apply to children as well?) hovered in the background throughout the whole genesis of the UN Convention on the Rights of the Child.

1. A short history

Around the turn of the century a considerable degree of interest in child protection was already evident (including on the part of legislators). Just about everywhere in the industrialised world so-called 'child-protection' and 'compulsory education' laws were passed. The book "The Century of the Child", published in 1903 by Ellen Key, a Swedish feminist, was a resounding success and widely read, even outside the narrow circle of reform-educationalists. This international attention to children was also expressed in new rules. In 1902 the Hague Conference on Private International Law considered "the interest of the child" as an important criterion in the convention on guardianship of minors. In 1919 the ILO (International Labour Organisation) adopted a convention which set a minimum age for employing children in industry. Despite the fact that these rules apply internationally, it is the Geneva Declaration (1924) which is regarded as the first international (human) rights instrument dealing with the rights of children.

It is quite clear that the new Convention (1989) was strongly influenced both by the changes in child-image, which occurred at the end of the twentieth century, and by the human rights project (see chapter 3). In this short history of international instruments dealing with children's rights, the reader will notice how their development is an illustration of the changes described above.

1.1. Geneva Declaration (1924)

The Geneva Declaration is clearly a defensive instrument by virtue of its origin. The First World War had left millions of children in deplorable circumstances. In 1920 Eglantyne Jebb, president of the Save the Children Fund and the International Red Cross Committee decided to set up the *Save the Children International Union*. This international organisation soon had numerous national sections dealing with the (post-war) plight of children.

For our purposes the important thing is that the five fundamental aims of the organisation were put in a five-points-programme called the "Declaration of the Rights of the Child":

1. The child must be given the means needed for its normal development, both materially and spiritually.
2. The child that is hungry should be fed; the child that is sick should be helped; the erring child should be reclaimed; and the orphan and the homeless child should be sheltered and succoured.
3. The child must be the first to receive relief in times of distress.
4. The child must be put in a position to earn a livelihood and must be protected against every form of exploitation.
5. The child must be brought up in the consciousness that its best qualities are to be used in the service of its fellowmen.

In simple terms (there is in fact no reference to rights as such) the Declaration points out adults' obligations to children. The child was protected as a person with his/her own rights, but remained dependent on adults to assert the rights included in the Declaration.

Although in content it also takes a defensive line on the consequences of the First World War (physical neglect, malnutrition, interrupted education, economic exploitation, ...), the Declaration does go further. It stresses social and economic needs (rights), over and above traditional civil and political rights.

In 1924 the Declaration was adopted and solemnly proclaimed in the General Assembly of the League of Nations. Since then it has been known as the Geneva Declaration (Appendix I).

Ten years later, in 1934, the Declaration was reconfirmed by the League of Nations' General Assembly and the states 'promised' to enact its principles in their own legislation.

For the first time ever, because of the Declaration, children's rights became a concept in public international law (albeit in the form of "soft law"), The Declaration was to become the cornerstone of all future international legislative initiatives regarding children's rights.

1.2. Declaration of the Rights of the Child (1959)

1.2.1. *Preparation and unanimous adoption*

Immediately after the Second World War, attempts were made to have the earlier Geneva Declaration adopted, and thereby reconfirmed, by the United Nations, which had been set up in the meantime. For this purpose, ECOSOC (the UN Economic and Social Council), whose responsibilities include the Commission on Human Rights, consulted the member states and a number of Non-Governmental Organisations. In the light of reactions received and of the preparations for the Universal Declaration of Human Rights (1948) already under way, it was decided that the Geneva Declaration would be considered good basis for discussion, needing change and extension, in view of changing attitudes to children's rights.

In 1950 a new draft was put to the Commission on Human Rights. Because of pressure of work caused by two human rights conventions (not adopted until 1966, see above), it was 1957 before the Commission was able to start dealing with the draft declaration. After consulting the member states, and extensive preparatory work by the Commission, the Declaration of the Rights of the Child was finally unanimously adopted by the then 78 members of the UN General Assembly in the form of resolution 1386 (XIV) (Appendix II).

Because of this exceptional unanimity – not even the Universal Declaration of Human Rights had been adopted unanimously – the Declaration had more moral authority than other soft laws.

1.2.2. *Content*

Compared to the Geneva Declaration, this Declaration is far more precise, and the earlier content and principles have been considerably widened.

It refers not only to the tangible needs of the child, but also to the need for love and understanding. It stresses the need to keep families together, that of pre and postnatal care for mother and child, and the principle of the right to a name and nationality. The principle of compulsory and free primary education is also included. Exploitation of children is opposed by a more specific set of provisions banning child labour under a certain age, and reinforced by the institution of the right to play and recreation.

In practical terms, apart from the preamble, the 1959 Declaration contains 10 principles, summarised below:

1. Every child shall enjoy all the rights set forth in the Declaration without any form of discrimination.
2. The child shall enjoy special protection and shall be given opportunities to develop in a healthy and normal manner, and in conditions of freedom and dignity.
3. The child shall be entitled from birth to a name and nationality.
4. The child shall enjoy the benefits of social security, including adequate pre- and post-natal care both for him and for his mother. The child shall have the right to adequate nutrition, housing, recreation and medical services.
5. The child who is physically, mentally or socially handicapped shall be given special treatment, education and care.
6. The child shall, where possible, grow up in the care and under the responsibility of his parents, in an atmosphere of affection, and of moral and material security. A child of tender age shall not, save in exceptional circumstances, be separated from his mother. Society and the public authorities shall extend particular care to children without a family and to those without adequate means of support.
7. The child is entitled to receive education, which shall be free and compulsory, at least in the elementary stages. The child shall have full opportunity for play and recreation.

8. The child shall in all circumstances be among the first to receive protection and relief.
9. The child shall be protected against all forms of neglect, cruelty and exploitation. The child shall not be admitted to employment before an appropriate minimum age.
10. The child shall be protected from racial, religious and any other form of discrimination. He shall be brought up in a spirit of understanding, tolerance and friendship among peoples, peace and universal brotherhood.

In the preamble explicit reference is made to children's physical and mental immaturity, which entitles them to special care and attention, including legal protection, both before and after birth. Hence, and this is exceptional (see below: horizontal effect), parents, men and women individually, voluntary organisations, local authorities and national governments are called upon to recognise these rights and to ensure their implementation, by enacting legislation, or in other ways.

1.2.3. *Some features*

Below we discuss those features of children's rights which are most relevant to our subject matter.

a) Child image: shift from legal object to legal subject

The Geneva Convention still regards children merely as objects of the law: "... the child must be given ...". The UN Declaration departs from this viewpoint and takes the first steps towards recognition of children as legal subjects (people with their own rights): "The child shall enjoy all the rights set forth in this Declaration". In the text we see a shift of emphasis from welfare and protection of the child to the protection of the *rights* of the child. The vocabulary no longer sounds naive, and has become more legal in nature.

Although the Declaration regards the child as a *legal subject*, it does not recognise his/her *competence* to exercise his/her rights independently. The Declaration deals almost exclusively with *protective rights*, the leitmotif being *the best interests of the child*; the child as separate entity in other words. During preparation of the Declaration the desirability of this separate declaration was a subject of discussion. There was already the Universal Declaration of Human Rights after all. Was there any real need for a specific declaration for children? It was however the general feeling that the Universal Declaration needed to be "complemented" by a series of specific declarations. The Declaration of the Rights of the Child was meant to be just such a specific declaration, because of children's special needs.

b) Normative value

First of all we have to note the fact that individuals in general (and therefore also children), for the protection of their rights in international law depend upon the implementation of international rules in their national legal system. If there is no implementation, or it is insufficient international rules are of very little use.

Furthermore, a declaration is merely a moral code, with no binding effect.

A number of principles in the 1959 Declaration are also to be found in other important human rights instruments. The fact that it is possible to invoke the principles of the Declaration through these legally binding treaties, has led some to say that the 1959 Declaration also would have a binding effect (there have been court rulings which have used this rationale). This also underlines the moral value of the Declaration for those states which have not ratified the 1959 Declaration.

The real legal base for the Declaration is said to be the UN Charter (the Constitution of the UN), which has obviously been ratified by all UN member states. Although there is no clear list of all recognised human rights in the Charter, article 68 establishes a Commission on Human Rights, with the task of drafting a Bill of Rights. The 1948 Universal Declaration and the 1966 Covenants are the most impressive results so far. The Declaration of the Rights of the Child can also be regarded as a part of this human rights project in the Charter.

Looked at in this light, the fact that the 1959 Declaration was unanimously approved is a strong argument in favour of its normative value. In fact, this unanimity reflects a consensus reached both on formulation of the principles and on their interpretation.

Obviously, the fact that a number of principles pertinent to children's rights are already contained in important international treaties is a further strong argument for the normative value of the Declaration. We have already referred to the 1919 International Labour Organisation Convention on the minimum age for certain kinds of labour. After 1919 the ILO drafted other international treaties containing binding rules on children's rights. The 1949 Red Cross Conventions and its protocols, have already been mentioned, these too contained specific rules on children. The same applies to a number of regional treaties, such as the European Convention on Human Rights, which clearly considers children's rights binding, as demonstrated by its rules and by court rulings. An analysis of all relevant international (human rights) instruments would take us too far.

However, the two 1966 Covenants, which aimed to make Universal Human Rights binding, are extremely important in this context. Both Covenants in the text refer to the status of the child, and indeed devote several passages to it. It is also worthy of note that during preparation for the International Covenant on Civil and Political Rights there was a fierce debate on the need for a separate and therefore specific article on the rights of the child. Opponents felt it was sufficient to refer to the non-discrimination principle contained in articles 2 and 26; in other words they felt human rights to apply to children too. In the end a specific article (article 24) was included. The debate in the Commission on Human Rights was one of the reasons for deciding, in preparation of the 1959 Declaration, not to adopt binding rights for children. Poland, together with a number of other states, had argued in favour of drafting a binding convention rather than a declaration. This would have forced the states parties to respect children's rights by bringing national legislation into line with the convention. As we know, in 1959 the time was not yet ripe for this. It is however important to know that the title of the original draft was "UN Charter on the rights of the child". Israel, particularly, was adamant this title should be maintained. The US were against, precisely because this would have led to a legally binding instrument.

The main impetus to starting work on the Convention on the Rights of the Child came not only from this fundamental debate on the question of the need for separate children's rights, and on the normative effect of the Declaration but also from the confusion engendered by the increasing number of international human rights instruments (at the moment they number about 80), each containing scattered references to the status of children.

In conclusion, we can say that the normative effect of the 1959 Declaration was limited. It was more important as a guideline for our relationship with children and as a frame of reference (rather than a legal standard) for evaluating this relationship. It was first and foremost a weapon in the struggle to improve the position of young people in society, both for voluntary organisations and the authorities.

c) Horizontal effect

A special characteristic of the 1959 Declaration is that its principles are considered to have horizontal effect. What does this mean?

As is generally known, the UN General Assembly is one of the bodies of an international intergovernmental organisation. It is only to be expected therefore that it address itself in the first place, if not exclusively, to (member) states or the institutions of other international organisations. Not so the 1959 Declaration. The Declaration, in its preamble, not only calls upon government bodies, but also upon parents, individuals and voluntary organisations to recognise children's rights. Individuals, rather than governments, are responsible for its implementation. This is what we call the horizontal effect of the Declaration.

1.3. Genesis of the Convention on the Rights of the Child (1959-1989)

1.3.1. *The United Nations System*

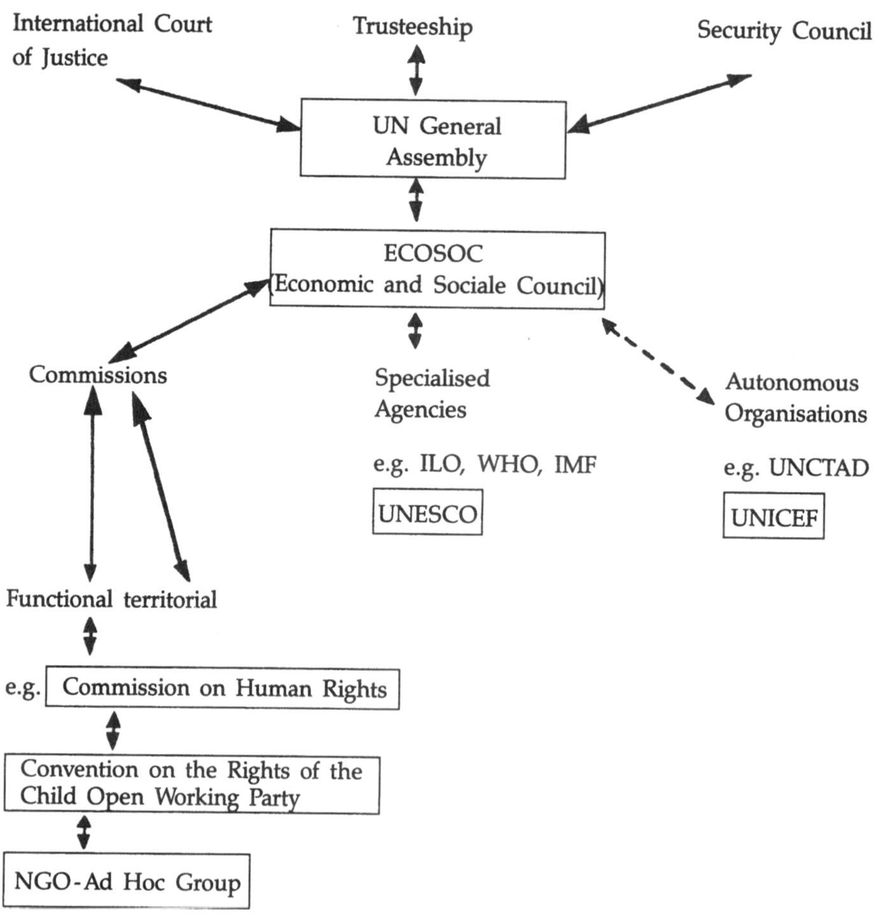

Before discussing how the Convention on the Rights of the Child came about, let us briefly examine the way the UN functions and in particular the procedure for adopting Conventions.

The United Nations are an organisation of sovereign nations and not a world government. As an inter-governmental organisation, it provides structures to help find solutions for disputes and problems and for joint action in practically every question concerning humankind, as contained in the Charter.

For the realisation of human rights treaties, the most important bodies are the General Assembly and the Economic and Social Council (ECOSOC).

All members of the UN have a seat in the General Assembly, the UN's central organ, which formally adopts international treaties, to be signed and ratified by the members. For substantive matters a two thirds majority of members present is required, less important decisions being taken by simple majority. Every member state has one vote.

The Economic and Social Council (ECOSOC) deals with economic, cultural and humanitarian co-operation and is also responsible for human rights issues. ECOSOC makes recommendations on these matters and drafts treaties to be put to the General Assembly. It can also call international conferences on matters within its purview. Furthermore, it can set up special commissions. Examples of such commissions are the Regional Commissions (set up on a geographical basis) and the Functional Commissions, such as the Commission on Human Rights. The Commission on Human Rights is made up of government representatives, who meet annually to examine infringements of human rights and fundamental freedoms in different countries and territories.

It is also part of ECOSOC's mandate to co-ordinate the activities of the specialised agencies. These are organisations which came about as the result of treaties and, legally speaking, are autonomous. The ILO and UNESCO are examples of such organisations. The ILO (International Labour Organisation) drafts conventions and programmes to improve the living and working conditions of workers. It establishes international standards to be used by national authorities in implementing conventions. It carries out an extensive technical co-operation programme to provide governments with technical assistance in implementing labour policy, and also engages in training, education and research. The main objective of UNESCO (United Nations Educational, Scientific, and Cultural Organisation) is to contribute to world peace and security by promoting co-operation between nations through education, science, culture and communication. Both organisations report to ECOSOC and are UN financed.

The ILO and UNESCO should not be confused with UN Autonomous Bodies such as UNICEF and UNCTAD. These are still more independent of the UN, with their own budget from voluntary contributions. These organisations have only formal links with the General Assembly and do not report to ECOSOC. Originally, the main objective of UNICEF (United Nations Children's Fund) was to help children in post-war Europe (in 1946 UNICEF stood for United Nations International Children's Emergency Fund). These days UNICEF links humanitarian aid with development and co-operates with developing countries in their efforts to protect children and give them the opportunity of developing their full potential.

UNICEF was one of the organisations which contributed to the Convention on the Rights of the Child, even though the Convention was drafted by ECOSOC's Commission on Human Rights. The actual drafting work was carried out by a working party of the Commission on Human Rights, in which NGO's were for once allowed to play a part (see below).

To sum up, UN Conventions are prepared by ECOSOC, or one of its ancillary organisations, and put to the General Assembly for adoption.

The actual preparatory work is done by many working parties (committees). Once texts been filtered through ECOSOC, they are then formally adopted by the General Assembly.

1.3.2. *The Polish initiative*

The reader will remember that during preparations for the 1959 Declaration, it was mainly Poland which, along with a number of other members, argued for a convention rather than a declaration. On 7th February 1978 it was once again Poland which put a draft Convention on the Rights of the Child to the Commission on Human Rights. The Polish government wanted to celebrate the International Year of the Child, proclaimed by the UN in 1979, to commemorate the 20th anniversary of the Declaration, by adopting a *separate* children's rights convention.

The Polish draft was almost word for word the text of the Declaration, albeit updated and with some additions. For instance, in the preamble, a reference to the 1966 Covenants, in the meantime in force, had been added. The text also contained articles on monitoring (duty of the states parties to submit reports), ratification, procedure for entry into force, etc.

The Commission on Human Rights, however, decided to consult member states and competent organisations. There were 28 responses from members, 4 from specialised agencies (ILO, IMF, UNESCO, WHO) and 15 from non-governmental organisations (surprisingly, UNICEF, a specialised agency, did not reply). Although responses varied, both on what should be covered and on the procedure, no state objected to the idea of a convention. It was felt, however, that the 1979 deadline could not be met.

We will now give a brief description of the responses and of the reasons why preparations for a convention were started.

- First of all, it was noted that between 1959 and 1978 numerous instruments had been adopted which, in one way or another, referred to the status of children. Some of them were binding, others not. References to children were scattered over international, regional and bilateral legislation. Moreover the terminology used often varied from one text to another, referring to children, youth, young people, minors, adolescents, etc. There were also overlaps and inconsistencies between the various international instruments. It was widely felt that there was therefore a need for something to be done, hence the idea of a convention (20 years on).
- In addition, it was felt the Polish draft stuck too closely to the 1959 Declaration.
  It was also not clear whether the text would have self-executive force.
- There had been fundamental changes in ideas on the position of children, and more and more people recognised the need to improve the legal situation of children (see above).
- There was the fundamental issue of what the content of such an international convention should be. In other words: what should be covered by a separate convention and, yet again, the fundamental question was raised of whether human rights should or should not apply to children.

1.3.3. *The Open Working Party and the NGO Ad Hoc Group*

On the basis of the responses received (summarised by the UN Secretary-General in a report submitted to the Commission on Human Rights on 27th December 1978), the Commission decided to set up a working party, with the job of drafting a convention. This working party was to be an *open working party,* allowing states who are not a member of the Commission on Human Rights, to take part in its work.

Although originally the Polish text was used as an initial draft, it was gradually replaced by *NGO texts*. This is unique in the history of the UN. It may become a precedent for other important legal instruments (e.g. the so-called third generation of human rights, see UNCED conference in Rio).

The international non-governmental organisations (numbering about thirty), for their part, had set up an *Ad Hoc Group* in 1983, to enable them to co-ordinate texts and optimise lobbying activities in the member states. It was to be this group which gave new impetus to the activities which had nearly ground to a halt after 1979. Defence for Children International (DCI) set up in 1979, International Year of the Child, by J. Moerman, a Flemish canon, was to act as their secretariat and UNICEF provided logistical and other support, thus becoming involved in the drafting process (this time). The number of members of the Ad Hoc Group kept increasing, and by 1989 had risen to 50. Later on, even after the adoption of the Convention, the group was to go on playing an extremely important role in the process of signing, ratifying, implementing, and monitoring the Convention. *The NGO Group for the Convention on the Rights of the Child* currently co-ordinates the national coalitions on children's rights (see above).

1.3.4. *The different draft texts*

The Open Working Party had been asked to grant the highest priority to work on the draft convention, so that it could be adopted in the International Year of the Child (1979). It soon became clear this deadline could not be met.

Given the issues involved and the way they were to be tackled, there would not have been time to present a balanced text acceptable to everybody involved. It was therefore decided to do a thorough job and allow more time for the preparatory work.

a) Draft Convention at first reading

In 1980 a second text (the first being the Polish) was drawn up, yet again without fundamental changes to the concept. The articles had been drafted in such a way, however, that they became obligations on states, and the child was no longer the central subject, i.e. the main point of principle in the debate was now absent from the text. It may well have been the very fact that this issue (do human rights also apply to children?) was so fundamental that prevented its being. No real thought was given to the basic principles of the content of the convention, and the Open Working Party contented itself with a critical appraisal of parts of the text.

But the very fact that there was no joint viewpoint on the principles to be contained in the convention made it possible to introduce any kind of amendments or to extend the articles. The fundamental issue did however crop up in the debate with great regularity throughout the whole drafting process.

Drafting work progressed slowly and laboriously. (The Open Working Party met only once a year, for a week).

There are different reasons why drafting in the end took a little more than ten years.

- As we have said, the Commission on Human Rights Open Working Party met only once a year.
- There were numerous proposals and counterproposals on the draft.
- The number of participants to the discussions increased gradually, each with their own ideas.
- There are many elements to children's rights: political, civil, economic, social and cultural rights all had to be discussed.
- Many different legal and cultural traditions were involved, and therefore long discussions were needed to reach a consensus.
- There was also the discussion on which rights were children's rights ...
- Finally there was the language problem.

Many different proposals were submitted and each discussion in turn led to further changes. Because of all this chopping and changing and because there was no real deadline, it seemed as if the process might go on for years. It became clear that it would be necessary to fix a finishing point, a target date. This became 1989, 10 years after the International Year of the Child and 30 years after the Declaration of the Rights of the Child. During the meeting of the Open Working Party in 1988 agreement was reached on the Draft Convention at first reading.

b) Draft Convention "at second reading"

At the end of 1988 the Ad Hoc Group submitted a text for discussion to the Open Working Party (second reading). It had already been through a technical reading (i.e. checked for internal and external contradictions).

Again this text led to much debate (67 working papers were submitted!).

It soon became clear, however, that in order not to endanger consensus, the Open Working Party would have to revert to the version of the text approved at first reading.

However, yet again an attempt was made, by West Germany this time, to state explicitly that human rights apply to children. At the very least, it was felt reference should be made to the fact that general human rights instruments cover children. The proposal was rejected once more, and the issue not debated.

In this way the Convention became the result of a delicate balancing act between numerous proposals. The final result was a well-prepared text, which therefore in 1989 sailed through both the next sessions of the Open Working Party and the Commission on Human Rights without friction or further controversy.

It is obvious that through all this drafting difficulties that the content of the Convention is only a *minimum* (consensus) *standard*. The drafters of the Convention must be aware of it, since they they drafted a separate article (article 41) in which is enshrined the principle that, if any standards set in national or international law are higher than those of this Convention, it is the higher standard that applies.

2. Content of the Convention

On 8th March 1989, at its 45th session, the UN Commission on Human Rights decided to submit the draft convention on the Rights of the Child to the General Assembly, via ECOSOC. On 20th November 1989 the Convention was adopted without a dessenting vote by the General Assembly, in its resolution 44/25. It was to enter into force after ratification by at least 20 countries (see below).

Thus the text evolved from a declaration (1924) made up of a preamble and five points, to a declaration (1959) with a preamble and 10 principles, to a convention (1989) with an extensive preamble (13 paragraphs) and no less than 54 (!) separate articles (see annexe III).

The preamble contains the main principles of the Convention. The articles can be subdivided into three main parts:

1) art. 1-41: the substantive articles, defining the rights of the child and obligations on states parties ratifying the convention.
2) art 42-45: procedures for monitoring implementation of the Convention
3) art. 46-54: formal provisions governing entry into force of the Convention.

Below we shall briefly examine the content of the preamble and the three parts of the Convention.

2.1. Preamble

A preamble (i.e the introduction to most, if not all, international conventions) explains the background to, and the reasons for, the convention. Hence the preamble does not contain binding principles, but gives a frame of reference, in the light of which the articles are to be interpreted.

The preamble to the Convention on the Rights of the Child refers to:
- the principles of the UN Charter (1945), the Universal Declaration of Human Rights (1948) and the International Covenants on Human Rights (1966);
- the conviction that families should be afforded special protection, and that children should grow up in a family environment, in an atmosphere of happiness, love and understanding;
- the conviction that the child should be brought up in the spirit of the ideals proclaimed in the UN Charter, and in particular in the spirit of peace, dignity, tolerance, freedom, equality and solidarity;
- bearing in mind the need to extend particular care to children, as stated in the Geneva Declaration on the Rights of the Child (1924), and the Declaration of the Rights of the Child (1959), as recognised in the Universal Declaration of Human Rights (1948), International Covenants on Human Rights (1966), several other conventions and the statutes of specialised agencies and other declarations (such as the 1985 Beijing Rules on the Administration of Juvenile justice);
- recognition that there are children living in exceptionally difficult conditions, and that such children need special consideration;
- the importance of tradition and peoples' cultural values in protecting children and ensuring their harmonious development;
- the importance of international co-operation.

2.2. Rights guaranteed by the Convention: comprehensiveness!

The rights guaranteed by the Convention are covered by articles 1 to 41. Here we find all those individual or operational articles dealing with the rights of children or others' obligations to them.

Considering each article separately would be too much. Furthermore, a subdivision of rights into different categories would be in breach of the spirit of the Convention, which makes no distinction between the different rights, and establishes no hierarchy. Indeed, the intention of bringing them all together in one *comprehensive instrument* was precisely to indicate that they were all equally important and even interdependent. In other words, none of these rights can stand alone. Respect for human dignity moreover requires this. The comprehensiveness of the Convention on the Rights of the Child is underlined especially by the fact that both first-generation and second-generation human rights have been brought together here. This is unique in the history of human rights (see the two separate international covenants of 1966). This emphasises the indivisibility and the non-hierarchy of these rights.

In view of the particular vulnerability of children, the Convention also contains the protection of children against abuse and exploitation. In addition, specific rights are formulated for special groups of children and children in special circumstances. In all this, the Convention also aims at ensuring that the views of children are always taken into account.

Indeed, this is the first recognition of children's participatory rights by an international regulation. In short, looked at from various angles, the Convention on the Rights of the Child can be said to be all-embracing or comprehensive.

Before discussing them in groups, we must mention a number of important general provisions.

2.2.1. *General provisions*

First of all, in article 1 we find the definition of the child: "For the purposes of the present Convention a child means every human being below the age of 18 years". This text also contains the extremely complex and delicate procedure, for reconciling opposing views on protection of the child before birth (explained in the preamble with a text between inverted commas).

It is debatable, of course, whether an international convention, involving 159 countries, is a suitable instrument for attempting to agree on an issue which still causes division within many countries.

Inconceivable big exception on this 18 years as the general age-level, is to be find in article 38, on the involvement of children in armed conflicts and their recruitement into the armed forces. Here the age level is determined on 15 years! Already during the drafting proces of the Convention the debate on this issue was very heated. Thanks to the enormous efforts and lobbying of NGO's, an optional protocol could be adopted by the UN General Assembly on 25 May 2000. The protocol raises the age from 15 to 18 for the involvement of children in armed conflicts, unfortunately however not for the recruitement into the army (Appendix IV).

We must also mention article 3, which states that the *best interests of the child* must be the primary consideration in all decisions concerning the child, and that the state must provide appropriate assistance if parents, or others legally responsible, fail in their duties.

In this context, articles 5 and 18 are also extremely important. Article 5 stipulates that states undertake to respect the right and responsibility of parents to provide direction and guidance in the exercise by the child of the rights recognised in the Convention. In addition, article 18 states that both parents are jointly responsible for the upbringing and development of the child. The state undertakes to render appropriate assistance where necessary.

2.2.2. *Possible subdivisions*

a) Traditional subdivision of human rights.

The rights of the child, recognised by the Convention, can be subdivided in five headings in line with the traditional classification of human rights:

1) Civil rights
   In general, these correspond to the rights recognised by the first 18 articles of the Universal Declaration of Human Rights (1948). Examples are the right to a name and to acquire a nationality (article 7) and the right to an identity (article 8); the right to life (article 6) and the principle of non-discrimination (article 2). But there are also the so-called "integrity rights", such as the ban on torture (article 37), the right to protection from physical violence (articles 19 and 34), from arbitrary arrest (articles 37 and 40), the right to privacy (article 16), ...

2) Political rights
   These cover freedom of opinion (article 12), freedom of expression (article 13), freedom of association (article 15), freedom of opinion, religion and conscience (article 14), freedom of access to information (article 17). Note should be taken that in the Universal Declaration the heading Political Rights also covers the right to vote and the right to stand for election.

3) Economic rights
   Article 4 states in general terms that states parties shall take all appropriate legislative, administrative and other measures regarding economic, social and cultural rights. More specifically this involves, among other things, the right to be protected from exploitation (articles 32 and 36).

4) Social rights
   Again article 4. This heading also covers the right to education (articles 28 and 29), health care (article 24), and social security (article 26).

5) Cultural rights
   In addition to article 4 once again, in this context we need to mention article 31, recognising the right to rest and leisure, to engage in play and to participate fully in cultural and artistic life.

The rights recognised by the Convention clearly coincide with traditional human rights.

b) Subdivision according to objectives

The Convention has 3 main objectives:

1) Right of Self-determination
   A number of universal human rights are now explicitly recognised and therefore confirmed as applying to children. This was uncontroversial in the case of certain rights, such as the right to protection from torture. Others were much contested (see above on debate during preparation of the Convention).
2) Right to protection
   The Convention contains a number of provisions addressing the special needs of children and especially of their vulnerability, e.g. conditions of employment for children (article 32). A number of these provisions impose more stringent requirements in the case of children than general human rights instruments.
3) Specific rights
   There are rights which apply specifically or even exclusively to children: the right not to be separated from their parents (articles 9, 10 and 11), and provisions regarding adoption (article 21). The best example under this heading is article 31, recognising the right to engage in play.
   The Convention also aims to afford protection for specific categories of children: refugees (article 22), handicapped children (article 23), minorities (article 30) and children caught up in armed conflicts.

c) The three P's

It is possible to subdivide in other ways, e.g. one commonly used, the 3 P's.

- Provision: rights providing access to certain goods and services; the right to food and health care (articles 6 and 24), the right to education (articles 28 and 29), the right to enjoy social security (article 26), ...
- Protection: the right to be protected from certain activities; the right to be protected against maltreatment and neglect (article 19), the right to be protected from all forms of exploitation (articles 32 up to and including 36);

– Participation: the right to act in certain circumstances and the right to be involved in decision-making (articles 12 upto and including 17).

Especially article 12 is a key article. It recognises the right of the child to express an opinion, and to have that opinion taken into account in any matter or procedure affecting the child. Thus the Convention recognises the child as *having* an opinion and no longer as having a "not-yet" opinion.

Each subdivision throws a different light on the Convention. The first demonstrates that children have very few political rights. The three P's approach shows that the lion's share of their rights are to social services and protection. If one looks at the Convention from the point of view of its objectives, the right to self-determination is placed at the forefront.

It is also important to note article 41, which states that if provisions of the Convention coincide with those of other international laws, or the laws of states parties, it is in all circumstances those provisions offering the highest standard which shall take precedence. This is extremely important Because this convention, as is often the case, contains only minimum standards. This is the consequence of aiming at consensus between all the member states, or between as many as possible. The highest compromise therefore often equals the minimum standard.

This compromise characteristic of the Convention has already become apparent with regard to abortion (see above), but the same attitude can be seen with regard to the abolition of child labour. In fact, article 41 calls on every member state to do better than it is obliged to by the Convention.

The international community itself can also attempt to reinforce some of the weaker articles. This can be done for instance by designing *optional protocols*.

Already on 25 May, 2000 the General Assembly of the UN adopted two optional protocols to the Convention on the Rights of the Child. *The optional protocol on the sale of children, child prostitution and child pornography* provides a higher legal protection than enshrined in the articles 34, 35 and 36 of the Convention. *The optional protocol on involvement of children in armed conflicts* is raising the age from 15 (as it is now stated in article 38) to 18 as the minimum age to involve children in armed conflicts. Unfortunately no similar agreement could be reached for recruitement in the army (Appendixes IV and V).

Also other UN bodies can draft conventions which can provide higher legal protection to children. This is the case for instance with the *ILO-Convention 182* (1999) *on the abolition of the worst forms of child labour* (entry into force: 19 November 2000). This convention complements earlier ILO-conventions as well as article 32 of the Convention on the Rights of the Child.

3. Entry into force and monitoring

Although the articles on monitoring (articles 42-45) and entry into force of the Convention (articles 46-54) are obviously an integral part of it, we will deal with them separately from the substantive articles. This should not, however, be regarded as an implication that they are of less importance, as we shall soon see.

3.1. Entry into force

A convention can only become legally binding after certain conditions have been met. These conditions are indicated in the Convention. The Convention on the Rights of the Child, like other such texts, had also to complete the essential procedure of ratification by states parties. Ratification is the legal procedure, whereby the competent body of the state party – in most cases its Head of State – confirms the international agreement and accepts the obligations it imposes. Ratification involves a number of steps.

It goes without saying that the convention must first of all be adopted. The Convention on the Rights of the Child was adopted by the UN General Assembly on 20th November 1989, whereupon it was opened for signature, ratification or accession.

Owing to active lobbying by the NGO Group which had already been closely involved in drafting the text, during the official ceremony in New York on 26th January 1990 the Convention was immediately signed by 61 countries. In accordance with article 46, the Convention remained open for signature by other states.

However, signing a Convention entails no more than a moral obligation. By signing it, the state indicates its intention to ratify the convention and hence to take all necessary steps in line with national legislation. The state also accepts a moral obligation not to take measures in breach of the convention in the period between signature and formal ratification.

Obviously formal ratification is the more important step. In the case of the Convention on the Rights of the Child, instruments of ratification are lodged by States Parties with the UN Secretary General. Article 49, 2 states that the Convention shall enter into force in a particular country on the thirtieth day after that state lodges its instruments of ratification. Furthermore article 49, 1 states that the Convention will enter into force only on the thirtieth day following the date on which the twentieth set of instruments of ratification is lodged. Again owing, in part, to intensive lobbying by the NGO's, this minimum number was quickly reached, and on September 2nd 1990 the Convention officially entered into force.

Since that date it has been ratified by 191 other countries. Obviously the Convention remains open for accession or ratification by other states even now.

As we have said, after formal adoption of the Convention, the NGO Ad Hoc Group members began lobbying to speed up ratification (to reach the number of 20 ratifications as soon as possible). UNICEF and DCI played an important part in this process.

Article 51 stipulates that states are allowed to enter reservations on ratification, although reservations incompatible with the object and purpose of the Convention are not permitted. Making reservations is an extremely bad thing, because the standards in the Convention are only minimum standards (see above) and any reservations fundamentally undermine the universal nature of these standards.

It is also important to note that states parties may propose amendments. Any amendment adopted by a majority of states parties shall be submitted to the UN General Assembly for approval. When accepted by a two thirds majority of states parties, amendments become binding only on those states parties who voted in favour.

3.2. Monitoring

We have already said that conventions are so-called "hard law", in other words legally binding. When a state joins a convention (i.e. ratifies it), it enters into an international agreement with the other states parties. Along with the others, it accepts the obligation to put into practice the provisions of the convention. The legal principle "pacta sunt servanda" therefore also applies to international treaties between states.

A problem arising here, as in other areas of international law, is monitoring. Because there is no intergovernmental body (yet) effectively monitoring implementation of international law, each convention contains provisions on monitoring. In fact, if there is no provision for effective monitoring of a convention, it remains binding only on paper. Each convention being only as effective as its monitoring system. The Convention on the Rights of the Child also provides its own system to ensure implementation by states parties.

Because of its importance, monitoring will be discussed separately in Chapter 5.

4. Normative value of the Convention

As we have already said, most international conventions require transposition into national legislation, since they are binding only on states parties and not on their citizens. Directly applicable international conventions (such as the ECHR) are an exception to this rule: they can be invoked directly in national courts, without the need for national legislation.

We have already discussed the fact that the text approved in 1989 is a convention; unlike the 1959 Declaration, it is therefore binding on states parties, who have an obligation to implement the Convention within their own borders. If necessary, they must take legislative measures (article 4).

After accession to or ratification of the Convention, states may not make changes to their national legislation or introduce new legislation, if it would breach the Convention. At the beginning of 1992, moves to introduce heavier penalties for juvenile delinquents led to a strong protest movement in Western Australia. In this campaign, reference to international law (i.e. to the Convention on the Rights of the Child, already ratified by Australia) played a cardinal role.

The situation is different when individual citizens attempt to enforce rights guaranteed by the Convention in a national court. This is where the question arises of the Convention's *self-executive force*. Whether the Convention can be applied directly depends on a number of factors, including some outside the Convention itself. First of all to be directly enforceable in a national court the Convention must have been *ratified*. Therefore ratification of the Convention is important both in a national and in an international context. Secondly, the state involved must have recognised the principle of direct applicability of international conventions in its own legislation. States recognising this principle can express this in different ways. In certain countries (such as the Netherlands) direct applicability of international conventions is enshrined in the constitution; elsewhere, the principle has become part of case law (e.g. Belgium). Finally, the convention has to be suitable for direct application.

Therefore, to find out whether individuals can directly invoke the Convention on the Rights of the Child, we must examine the text more closely.

If a convention is to be directly applicable, its content must meet a number of conditions, e.g. it must be clear and comprehensive. If the text requires further elaboration before it can be used in a national court, this is work to be done by the national legislator.

Subjective rights guaranteed by the Convention will therefore be closely studied in every state party to determine whether they can be invoked directly. Because the terminology used in convention texts varies considerably, we must now take a closer look at terminological differences.

- *Binding declarations*
  In the Convention there are a number of provisions which are obviously legally binding. These are the provisions which can be invoked in court in those countries which recognise the Convention's direct effect. The text's binding nature comes out in expressions such as "recognise", "undertake", "respect", "ensure" and "guarantee". These expressions are used mostly in articles which confirm existing rights or freedoms (e.g. the non-discrimination principle in article 2).
- *Statements of intent*
  Provisions containing expressions such as "promote", "encourage", "use their best efforts", "strive" are to be considered statements of intent rather than binding measures.
- *Appropriate measures*
  Many provisions refer to undertakings by states parties to take "appropriate" measures. Terminology may even vary: "appropriate measures", "appropriate legislative and administrative measures", "appropriate legislative, administrative and other measures", etc.

The Convention on the Rights of the Child contains provisions referring both to first generation human rights and to those of the second generation. Hence the differences in terminology. Binding provisions refer to traditional first generation freedoms. They impose bans on states, requiring them to abstain from doing certain things. Provisions governing social, economic and cultural rights refer to positive obligations on states, which undertake to do certain things. These are so-called "appropriate measures".

We find the same terminological distinction between first and second generation human rights in other human rights instruments. The 1966 Covenant on Civil and Political Rights, for instance, contains mainly binding provisions, while the Covenant on Social, Economic and Cultural Rights refers mainly to intentions.

Attentive readers will have noticed that in some cases the three terminological categories appear in one and the same article. In the case of economic, social and cultural rights, for instance, there are both expressions entailing obligations for states parties and others calling for appropriate measures to be taken. We find the same combination in articles covering special categories of children. Where the Convention deals with specific rights, we find both declarations of intent and legally binding expressions.

Very often in the end it is case law which determines whether certain provisions can be invoked in national courts by individuals.

There is in fact not the same enthusiastic reception everywhere for the idea that the Convention should be directly enforceable. First of all, there are very few provisions which can be enforced directly. Secondly, those provisions which are binding seem to do very little more than reconfirm rights and freedoms already enshrined in other conventions: in other words they add nothing.

There is nothing wrong per se with reaffirming existing rights in a new convention. Indeed, in certain cases, provisions in the Convention on the Rights of the Child may shed new light on existing rights and freedoms.

The Convention does not, of course, exist in a legal vacuum. It is quite possible to invoke the Convention on the Rights of the Child *together* with other conventions. In this way, the Convention on the Rights of the Child can make an important contribution to legal practice. Fundamental rights, translated into national law can be refined and added to on the basis of its provisions. Article 12, quoted many times in this book, giving children the right to express their views in all matters which affect them, is an example of such a possible case.

Much depends on the willingness and creativity of lawyers and magistrates in making the Convention enforceable by individuals. In this sense, the theoretical debate on the Convention's normative value can lead to practical application of children's rights, through accurate and careful interpretation of the Convention.

Case law is expanding rapidly in a number of countries (see chapter 5), offering hope for the future.

5. Conclusion

If children were regarded as human beings, and it was therefore regarded as normal for human rights to apply to them, there would be no problems. In principle all human rights conventions would also apply to children. A separate convention on children's rights would be superfluous, because children could refer to existing instruments to assert their rights. However this is not the case.

If children's competence were generally recognised, it would be sufficient to add "age" as a non-discrimination criterion to existing human rights instruments. Article 14 of the ECHR, covering non-discrimination, offers ample possibilities to do so: the text contains a reference to "other status", which could also be read as meaning "children". Were the European Court for Human Rights to interpret or use article 14 in this way, the controversy over human rights and children would be considerably closer to being resolved. So far, however, this has not happened.

New universal and regional children's rights instruments are still being drafted while, simultaneously, both in law and in the courts, children's rights are gradually being integrated into existing human rights.

The Convention on the Rights of the Child does not state explicitly that human rights apply to children. However, for the first time in history, it does grant a number of fundamental human rights to children (articles 12 to 16). This recognition of fundamental human rights for children is an important new element in the debate on children's right to self-determination.

The debate on the distinction between human rights and children's rights is clearly still in its infancy. The Convention is not the final word, but only the beginnings of a solution, though at the same time it is an important strategic factor giving new impetus to the debate.

Generally, it is assumed human rights "in principle" also apply to children, but there is no agreement on the principle of children's legal competence.

In other words, the fundamental friction between *separate children's rights* and *general human rights* will be with us for some time to come.

Chapter 5

MONITORING

In this chapter we shall examine in more detail the procedure used for monitoring the Convention on the Rights of the Child.

The importance of international monitoring of the Convention's provisions has already been stressed. States Parties undertake to observe the Convention. By ratifying it, they undertake to implement its provisions in their country. For monitoring in a country, apart from the major task of issuing legislation, a prominent role must be played by the courts in those countries recognising the Convention's *self-executive force*. It has already been pointed out that in certain countries some of the Convention's provisions can be invoked directly in court, without the need for legislation. For instance, French case law has already established that article 12 can be applied directly. It has proved possible to have children's right to participate implemented in a state party by invoking this article in court. (On March 10th 1993 however, doubt was suddenly cast on this right by the – indeed extremely controversial – ruling handed down by the French Cour de Cassation which postulates that the Convention on the Rights of the Child cannot be directly invoked in a French court). In Belgium there have also been rulings which refer to the Convention. Already on April 20th 1993, a Juvenile Court judge in Mons decided in an appeal case to recognise minors as litigants in a civil law procedure by virtue of article 12 of the Convention. The ruling states that article 12 is clear and exhaustive enough for minors to be granted, on that basis, a subjective right to be heard in a legal action. In other words, article 12 is considered to have self-executing force.

The Convention entrusts monitoring of its implementation to a special ("treaty-based") body, the Committee on the Rights of the Child.

When examining monitoring, we therefore not only have to look at articles 42 to 45 of the Convention, but also at the experience of the Committee on the Rights of the Child, which was set up on February 27th 1991. Furthermore there are a number of quality criteria which can be used to test the Convention's monitoring mechanism.

1. Positive sanctioning

During preparation of the Convention, it was the NGO Ad Hoc Group which was particularly attentive to monitoring. The Ad Hoc Group considered it important to generate a "positive atmosphere" surrounding implementation. Contrary to the system used for monitoring in some other conventions (mostly based on confrontational measures and sanctions), the authors of the Convention on the Rights of the Child wanted to gain acceptance for the idea of mutual aid, assistance and co-operation. This idea is given shape explicitly in the substantive provisions of the Convention. Article 4, dealing with economic, social and cultural rights, states that states parties "shall undertake ... measures to the maximum extent of their available resources, and, where needed, within the framework of international co-operation." In fact experience had shown that accusations and sanctions were often counter-productive. All too often countries do not ratify international conventions from fear of being sanctioned for being unable to apply all the provisions (or unable to do so yet). This would inevitably be the case with something as far-reaching as the Convention on the Rights of the Child.

This is why the authors of the Convention on the Rights of the Child opted for advice and assistance to support implementation (see article 45, b and d). In other words, in their reports states parties can request technical advice and assistance to enable them to apply certain provisions of the Convention.

The downside of this approach might be that monitoring of this Convention does not therefore offer the same safeguards against infringements other Conventions have. For instance, there is no individual or interstate right to complain. Nor is there provision for taking disputes to the Committee on the Rights of the Child or to an International Court of Justice.

2. Committee on the Rights of the Child

2.1. Organisation

Article 43 provides for the establishment of a Committee on the Rights of the Child to monitor "progress made by states parties in achieving the realisation of the obligations undertaken in this Convention".

- Initial elections to the Committee were to be held no later than six months after the date of entry into force of the Convention, in other words before 2nd March 1991. The Committee was actually set up on 27th February 1991.
- The Committee is made up of 10 independent experts, serving in their personal capacity and not as representatives of a government or governmental organisation. They are elected by secret ballot. Each state party may nominate a candidate. The members of the Committee are elected for a four year term. Five members of the first Committee were chosen by lot to serve a term of two years.
  The number of members will probably be increased to eighteen very soon. The rather unexpected huge number of ratifications, reached at record speed (191 after 7 years) has resulted in a large influx of initial reports (as well as a some periodic reports already). This has meant a great increase of the Committee's work load. In 1995, Costa Rica submitted an amendment on the basis of article 50 to increase the number of members to eighteen. The General Assembly of the UN adopted this amendment in 1995 and it is now waiting for the required two-thirds majority of the states parties for it to come into force (article 50, 2). The number of notifications needed is 120. On 8 August 2000 only 91 were deposited.
- Within two years after ratification (and thereafter every five years) states parties have to report to the Committee on the Rights of the Child in their country (article 44, 1).
- The Committee may request further information from states parties (article 44, 4).
- The Committee may request studies on specific issues relating to the rights of the child (article 45, c).
- Every two years the Committee is to submit reports to the UN General Assembly through ECOSOC (article 44, 5).
- In order to foster effective implementation of the Convention and to encourage international co-operation in the field covered by the Convention, the Committee may, in accordance with article 45, invite specialised agencies, such as the ILO, the WHO, UNICEF, UNESCO, and non-governmental organisations to attend its meet-

ings. They can be asked for expert advice, or can themselves ask for information from the Committee.
- The Committee on the Rights of the Child is currently composed as follows:
  Doek, Jacob Egbert – Netherlands (1999-2003),
  El Guidi, Amina Hamza – Egypt (1999-2003),
  Fulci, Francesco Paolo – Italy (1997-2001),
  Karp, Judith – Israel (1995-2003),
  Rilantono, Lily – Indonesia (1997-2001),
  Mokhuane, Ester Margeret Queenie – South Africa (1997-2001),
  Quedrago, Awa N'Dey – Burkina Faso (1997-2003),
  Rabah, Ghassan Salim – Lebanon (1997-2001),
  Sardenberg, Marilla – Brazil (1997-2001),
  Tigerstedt – Tähtela, Elisabeth – Finland (1999-2003).

As indicated on 28 February 2001, the terms of five members of the Committee will expire. Elections for new members will be held during a meeting of States Parties on 26 February 2001.

There is a hope that the 120 notifications, nescessary to raise the number of the Committee members from 10 to 18 (cf. supra), will be deposited through wich the 8 additional experts could be elected at the same date. On 8 August 2000 (only) 91 notifications were deposited.

2.2. Guidelines

During its first meetings the Committee drafted a number of guidelines for states parties' initial reports on the implementation of the rights of the child in their country.

The first thing to be mentioned here is that the Committee attaches equal importance to all rights guaranteed by the Convention.

Moreover, in the guidelines, the Committee underlines 4 fundamental provisions, which are to be guiding principles for examining other articles:
- non-discrimination (article 2);
- best interests of the child (article 3);
- the right to life, survival and development (article 6);
- respect for the views of the child (article 12);

For the drafting of the report, the other articles were subdivided into different categories:
- General measures of implementation;
- Definition of the child;
- Civil rights and freedoms;
- Family environment and alternative care;

- Basic health and welfare;
- Education, leisure and cultural activities;
- Special protection measures.

The Committee expects each state party to measure the application of each provision by the yardstick of the four principles, making it possible to represent the reports by a two-dimensional diagram.

In this way, the Committee's guidelines complement and clarify the provisions of article 44, covering states parties' reports. It is important to note that article 44, 6 requires states parties to make their reports widely available to the public in their own country. In fact this is a direct result of article 42, requiring states parties to "make the principles and provisions of the Convention widely known, by appropriate and active means, to adults and children alike". That means that state parties have an *obligation to provide information* besides their *obligation to report* The Convention not only seeks to clarify whether children's rights are infringed. This specific provision clearly indicates that widespread knowledge of the rights of the child is the best protection against such infringements.

At its thirteenth meeting (October 1996), the Committee also drew up the General Guidelines for the periodic reports which have to be submitted every five years following the initial report. In fact, these guidelines are a more detailed (166 paragraphs!) elaboration of the guidelines for the initial reports, so that the emphasis is the same: the general fundamental principles, the comprehensiveness, and the non-hierarchic classification of the rights and therefore their interconnection. Naturally, the member state is explicitly asked for its reactions to the *concluding observations* formulated on the occasion of the initial report.

2.3. Operation

Below we will discuss a few aspects of the Committee's operation. It must be kept in mind that the Committee does not have a mandate to act as a sanctioning body. A major feature of all the Committee's activities remains the positive attitude to monitoring, aimed at a *constructive dialogue* with the convention states.

Initially, the Committee met only once a year (article 43,10) for a duration of three weeks. In view of the great work load, this has now been increased to three meetings per year, each time for three weeks. Its main task is the discussion of the country reports. Each meeting treats about six of these reports, which means that eighteen are dicussed every year.

In fact, every *report review* consists of two stages: a first discussion behind closed door in the so-called *presessional working group*, and three months after that, the actual *public session*.

At the meeting of the *pre-sessional working group*, the Committee also goes through any contributions from NGOs and compares them with the government report. Major key questions are drawn up and compiled in a supplementary list of issues which is sent to the state party. This gives it the opportunity to prepare itself better for the discussion at the plenary session.

After the report has been investigated, discussed and deliberated, the Committee publishes its findings, the so-called *concluding observations*. They are communicated to the General Assembly of the UN and of course to the state party in question, which is obliged to publish them together with the full report (article 44, 6). These concluding observations usually consist of five sections: (1) an introduction; (2) positive aspects; (3) factors and difficulties concerning the implementation of the Convention; (4) main reasons for concern; (5) suggestions and recommendations.

As such, the concluding observations are an extremely important document in the process of continuous monitoring, for they contain data which in turn form the starting points for the subsequent reports and discussions.

In addition to the investigation of the country reports, the Committee also takes on a number of supplementary tasks. Below, we will discuss: urgent actions, informal regional meetings, and specific studies.

– *Urgent actions* can be taken by the Committee in case serious circumstances require this. This can be done at the request of a state party or on the initiative of the Committee itself. The case in question must involve serious violations against the Convention on the Rights of the Child and must be based on reliable information. No procedure for urgent action has been used as yet.

– *Informal regional meetings* can be organised by the Committee with a view to promoting the Convention. These meetings are also a good opportunity for gaining more insight into the problems and possibilities of certain regions and countries. In addition to governmental authorities, NGOs and even children themselves can take part in these meetings. The insights gained as a result can be used adequately in the investigation of the country reports and can also be effective in the follow-up of the reports. Such meetings have already been organised in Latin America, Asia and Africa.

This task has recently been broadened and refined by the method of *missions*. A number of Committee members have been sent on missions to specifically chosen countries with a view to the ratification, effective implementation or the follow-up of the points identified during the discussion of the report.

Note that here too, the point is not *control*, but a constructive dialogue.

– In accordance with article 45,c, the Committee can request an *investigation* into specific themes connected to children's rights. The best-known studies are those on children in armed conflicts and on the commercial sexual exploitation of children. Both of them even gave rise to the process of developing optional protocols (see above).

In addition, the Committee organises an annual *theme or discussion day*. A discussion day is a kind of public hearing at which experts, representatives of intergovernmental and non-governmental organisations, and others, can make their findings, proposals, etc. known. This information can be important for tracing new developments and getting to know them better. They can also contribute to a more uniform and adequate interpretation of the Convention. Themes which have already been treated are: the economic exploitation of children, the role of the family, the girl-child, juvenile protection, the child and the media, children living in a world with HIV/aids, children with a handicap. For 2000 "state violence against children" will be discussed.

A very special task which the Committee has taken to heart is also implied in article 45, namely the possibility of providing technical advice and assistance to state parties. The best way to do this is in collaboration with the specialised organisations of the United Nations. To that effect, the High Commissioner for Human Rights designed an *Action Plan for Strengthening the Implementation of the Convention on the Rights of the Child* in 1995.

The plan provides for specific technical collaboration in six domains: (1) assistance with the preparation and drafting of the country reports; (2) experts mission in order to establish a general programme for technical collaboration with the government and others; (3) assistance with the revision and harmonization of national legislation; (4) assistance with the design or enhancement of the national monitoring and coordination mechanisms; (5) legal and practical assistance with the development of a national institute for children's rights; (6) training of professionals involved in working with children.

Unicef and the Centre for Human Rights are the main organisations of the UN which are involved in this plan. A similar programme is currently being developed with regard to juvenile protection.

On April 2000 there were 72 countries on the list for technical assistance. Among them 56 (80%) relate to juvenile justice.

Such a view of the task implied by article 45 also offers an opportunity for implementing article 4 *in fine*. In an unique way, it enables fresh and innovative *development co-operation*.

3. The report: an opportunity for pro-active implementation

It is clear that reporting is the Achilles' heel of the Convention. There is indeed a danger of the Convention being interpreted as a statement (of intent). The consequence would be that the Convention could not bring to light the contradictions in the society in which it is to apply. These contradictions would not become apparent until it was implemented, which, if it is done properly, will take *considerable effort*.

Generating greater respect for children and thus improving their living conditions is considered in the Convention to be an ongoing task. Looked at in this light, reporting can have an important function. It can become an instrument for promoting interest in, and discussion of children's rights in society at regular intervals (for the first time after two, then every five years). In this way, reporting becomes a sustainable means of actively improving children's situation.

Before this can happen, however, a number of important questions have to be answered: how will the report be drafted and by whom? What will go into it?

3.1. How and by whom?

Formally, the state is answerable to the Committee on the Rights of the Child for implementation of the Convention, in the same way as it is the state which, according to the provisions of the Convention, is responsible for implementing the rights guaranteed by it. This puts the state in the strange – but in international conventions not unusual – position of being judge and jury.

While it would be perfectly possible for the state to have civil servants draw up the report by arbitrarily stapling together documents from different departments, obviously this would show lack of respect.

Whereas, formally, reporting is a duty for the authorities, in actual fact implementation and monitoring are a *responsibility we all share*. Therefore monitoring should be conducted by an independent body.

The Convention is mostly phrased in terms of objectives rather than clearly defined rights, which is why a continuous dialectic process must be kept going.

Traditional ways of influencing decision-making, such as the right to vote, lobbying, market mechanisms, etc. do not work in the case of children. They need a new, different system for looking after their own interests and for exercising control over their own lives, especially since Parliamentary influence on the state has declined. And the state itself can hardly be regarded as an unbiased advocate of children's interests. The state has to take into account a whole range of interests, which do not always coincide with those of children.

Non-governmental organisations, already involved in drafting the Convention, have now made it clear that they intend to play an equally active part in monitoring. This is possible under article 44, 6 and article 45, which requires states to make their reports widely available in their own country. The Committee on the Rights of the Child has declared its intention to promote this watchdog-function and to be willing to accept criticism and supplementary information from NGO's (see above, the national and international coalitions).

Various proposals have already been put forward to create a structure to involve those active in the field. It would be possible, for instance, to copy the International Committee on the Rights of the Child structure nationally, or even at every relevant policy-level within the state, including locally.

This is where quality requirements come into play. These are the requirements to be met by any organisation which is to have the authority and durability needed to sustain a campaign focusing attention on children, thereby improving their position in society.

There are various ways in which these committees could give a voice to children, as a step towards making it the rule rather than the exception that children actively participate in all kinds of councils in all areas relevant to them. What children want most of all is respect. They want to be treated as people. And yet the *right to respect* and *to full citizenship* for children is still not the general norm. Children feel strongly their need to participate in the social debate. They have the feeling, however, that adults do not really listen to them. In many areas, their experience is that they are not taken seriously because they have no personal power, flowing from the right to vote or from paying taxes, and because it is assumed they are too immature to deal with serious matters. However children turn out to be quite capable of looking after themselves. They have important ideas and a considerable sense of responsibility. They lack opportunities to put these ideas into practice because the structures are not there. Children are offered very few opportunities to express and fulfil this part of themselves and to be taken seriously. They share a feeling of not really being able to influence the world around them.

Self-organisation, a right guaranteed by the Convention, poses legal problems. Children are not in a position to exercise their right to independence and self-determination. Adults are not always very patient when children try to assert their rights.

And yet children appear to have a number of *specific qualities* which could be useful to society: they are dynamic and capable of approaching most situations objectively, critically and with an open mind, since they are relatively independent of social institutions and interest groups. In this context, we have to attach great importance to the fact that respect for children's views, as enshrined in article 12, is regarded by the Committee on the Rights of the Child as a general principle. Article 12 guarantees children, able to form an opinion, the right to express that opinion on all matters affecting them. It also guarantees that those views will be given due weight. In order to put this right into practice, the article states that the child must be heard in all judicial and administrative proceedings affecting it. Against this background, it goes without saying that children should also be involved in monitoring the Convention.

In the end they are the experts par exellence in matters that affecting them. In this regard al lot can be expected from the *"What do You Think"*-project mentioned in chapter 2.

Several models haven been mooted for examining children's living conditions and monitoring implementation of the Convention:
- reports could be drawn up by states (as provided for by the Convention) and a standing committee responsible for follow-up could then examine them and suggest to the international experts' committee monitoring implementation of the Convention where critical questions might be asked.
- reports could be drawn up by states and a standing committee responsible for follow-up could, after critical consideration, recommend improvements to the report and to children's living conditions.
- reports could be drawn up by states which would invite a standing committee responsible for follow-up to recommend improvements to the report and to children's living conditions.

- the state could invite a standing committee responsible for follow-up to monitor children's living conditions (a task comparable to that of the international committee) and to act as co-authors of the report.
- within states parties this approach could be followed at different policy-making levels.

Whichever model is chosen, *the question arises as to the quality of monitoring both as a process and as a product*. It is absolutely essential for children's living conditions to be closely studied, if there is to be progress on them. This is also necessary to comply with the provisions on regular reporting by states.

3.2. Content

The formal question as to who draws up the report is not the only important one. We also have to ask what will go into it. One would expect there to be a straightforward answer to this question, but this is not the case. In a preceding chapter, we have already pointed out how limited our knowledge of children is. We know very little about their interpretations, about how they give meaning to events. There has been almost no research in this field. Moreover we lack even the simplest demographical data and what we have is out of date. This is also an area in which children could have a role to play, as research subjects. According to articles 12 and 13, children have the right to make their views known. Read in conjunction with article 17, these provisions also grant children the right, as consumers of information, to be informed on what data have been collected about them and to make known their reservations if any. Moreover research from the viewpoint of adults, using the child as unit of observation (a children's ethnography) could bring us closer to understanding children's position in social structures, and thus contribute to a debate on the subject. Our knowledge of children is also fragmentary, because it covers only those areas considered relevant by adults. For a long time, it was assumed our knowledge of children was extensive, but gradually we are becoming aware that it is limited and directed mostly at problem areas. We have begun to realise there is an almost complete absence of the kind of data considered relevant by children. Again the *"What do you think"*-project can play an important role in it.

3.3. Quality requirements

If a structure is to carry out the above-mentioned tasks, it will have to comply with strict quality standards. These standards have been examined in a study carried out by the Belgian King Baudouin Foundation in 1991.

3.3.1. *General quality requirements*

1. The intention of articles 44, 6 and 45 is to provide a broad foundation for monitoring within society. The *development of networks* in the field of children's rights is encouraged and regarded as an important quality requirement for monitoring. Networks, both of children and of adults, are extremely important for maintaining the momentum of our attention to and action on behalf of children's rights. Networks are essential as sources of information, as support for individual initiatives and as instruments for a smooth and rapid exchange of information. Children also have to be put in a position to share their experiences with other children, and particularly with children from other cultures.

2. At the moment the issue of children's position in society is receiving a great deal of attention. More and more interest is shown in the rights of the child. We can learn a lot from the experience of adult projects aimed at improving the position of children. This is the kind of project we most frequently encounter and is very much in line with the spirit of the Convention (the best interests of the child being the guiding principle). Proper monitoring will have to take into account the experience of *child advocacy.*

3. Our attitude to children appears to have considerable impact on the way we interpret children's rights and judge the need for policy changes. Our child image determines our reaction to practical situations. At the moment in the West child images seem to be undergoing change. Data on the child as a social category and on children's views are therefore urgently needed. The *study of the child* will therefore be another important requirement for proper monitoring. The monitoring body will be faced with a number of difficult questions: is the child a person, in legal terms, or an object of others' desire and power? Do we have to regard the child as a creature to be protected by society, or as a partner with a full right to participate? Do we not all need protection, without this being regarded as a reason to deny us the right to participate? While the right of children to protection and well-being does not affect the balance of power between adults and children, freedoms do. A very solid case will therefore have to be put together if these rights are ever to be implemented in practice.

Present child images can roughly be subdivided into three categories, each stressing different actions to be taken:
- childhood can be considered as forming part of the private sphere and as a transition to adulthood. Here the stress will be on protection.
- children can also be regarded as a separate group, a permanent stratum of society. In this approach, childhood is seen as a social and political phenomenon and the focus is on the balance of power between adults and children. Policy will be directed at promoting independence.
- the intergenerational perspective stresses the need to study and balance the needs and views of different generations. Policy will therefore attach equal importance to protection and independence.

4. One of the changes in our child image which seems to be taking place is an increase in attention to children's assertiveness and participation, leading to more stress on the views and feelings of children themselves. Decision makers will have to start thinking about the need to promote children's participation. Experience acquired in the context of children's *self-organisation* will therefore be invaluable for monitoring (cfr. "What do You Think"-project).

The above-mentioned quality requirements are already in use in the strategies of the children's rights movement (see chapter 2). They are also regarded as key strategies in ombudswork. In order to assist implementation and thus to contribute to improving the position of children in society, these four key elements will also have to be called on when monitoring the Convention.

3.3.2. *Specific quality requirements*

1. Official status
   Conferring of official status would indicate acknowledgement of the need for special attention to the rights of children, and of the importance of the subject matter. It would equally demonstrate that the monitoring body was acknowledged as a permanent interlocutor.

2. Stability
   Stability can be achieved by anchoring the monitoring body in legislation, and by clearly defining its powers.

3. Authority and credibility
   Authority has to be founded on quality: the monitoring body has to display high standards of competence and performance. Its affir-

mations must be based on fact, not on hearsay, intuition or individual opinion. Making no statement at all is preferable to one with no basis in fact. Cases must be built on data obtained from multi-disciplinary research. Obviously this approach requires a great deal of factual knowledge. Wherever necessary, scientific help should be sought.

4. Impartiality and independence
   The monitoring body must deal exclusively with the rights of the child. The rights of the child have to be its focus, aim and sole point of departure. There must not be a hidden agenda, and other interests cannot be allowed to play a part. The debate must be lively and objective. No other interests may be served under the guise of promoting children's rights. Clashes of interest must be avoided at all costs. There must be no party political interference. Involvement in conflicts of individual families is also ruled out. The greatest possible autonomy and independence is essential. Nobody must be in a position to stop the monitoring body from dealing with a case. Autonomy need not however stand in the way of state recognition, which is desirable as an indication that the state also takes the view that monitoring children's rights is a necessity. Appointment of the monitoring body by an independent institution, such as Parliament, would offer immense advantages, guaranteeing both its autonomy and its authority. However, official recognition may not result in financial dependence. The monitoring body must be guaranteed proper funding, and sufficient staff for it to do its job properly.

5. Accountability
   Autonomy does not preclude accountability. However the monitoring body must be accountable only for fulfilling its general obligations and must be accountable directly to parliament.

6. Comprehensive nature
   The activities of the monitoring body must cover the whole of society, i.e. every aspect of the situation of children. The aim must be to achieve a full, integrated picture. In each and every case, the best interests of the child must be the prime consideration. Drawing up a list of potential tasks would serve only to limit its scope.

7. Approachability and openness
   If the monitoring body is to function as a catalyst and to enhance the debate in society, it must be an open institution, which can be

approached directly. It must have frequent contacts with individuals and organisations. Everybody, even the civil service, must have the right to approach the monitoring body in an informal manner. The monitoring body must also take into account the views of children themselves. Approachability and openness are all the more important in view of the monitoring body's task of being the voice of the child. It must be an open and friendly institution rather than an anonymous bureaucracy. It is also important for children to be put in a position to participate fully in monitoring their own living conditions.

8. Purposefulness
The number of activities is less important than their purpose. Activities have to aim at achieving practical results for children. This will require perseverance.

9. Broad powers
Among other things, the monitoring body must have far-reaching powers of inquiry, and therefore must have easy access to files and information. It must be able to require official bodies dealing with children to hand over information on request. If necessary confidentiality must be waived. The monitoring body must also have the right to be heard in all administrative activities relevant to children. Furthermore, it is important for the monitoring body to have full right of initiative, including that of making declarations on any subject at any time.

10. Confidentiality
If necessary, the monitoring body must have the right to protect its sources.

11. Relationship with the media
The monitoring body must pay special attention to its relationship with the media. It is important for it to become known in the right way, i.e. as a civic institution, concerned with human rights and dealing with children's competence rather than with problem cases. Such efforts in this direction must be ongoing and directed at each new generation, using inter alia the mass media in an attempt to target specific groups (parents, professionals, adults, etc.).

12. Realism
Ideal solutions may not be attainable, which is why they meet only

with general public indifference. A realistic attitude has far more chance of achieving an impact.

13. International co-operation
    It goes without saying that children's living conditions are not determined solely by what happens in their own country. To function effectively, what is done locally must go hand in hand with, and be inspired by, what is being done world-wide.

The quality requirements resulting from this study may well turn out to be very useful in stimulating national and regional (i.e. European) discussion on ways of using the Convention pro-actively, and particularly on monitoring.

Most of this quality requirements are met in established ombuds institutions like the Flemish Children's Rights Commissioner.

Chapter 6

PRACTICAL CONSEQUENCES OF THE CONVENTION

In preceding chapters we have discussed a number of characteristics of the Convention. We have described its comprehensive nature and its instrumental function, and pointed out a number of ways in which the Convention can have a positive impact. The aim of bringing together different categories of rights in one instrument was to demonstrate their equal importance, and even interdependence.

In this chapter, we shall take another look at the Convention's characteristics, and their practical consequences in a number of areas particularly relevant to children. We will examine what the benefits can be for education, social assistance, child labour and the media. These areas have been chosen as *examples of areas* where the Convention may have beneficial effects in the struggle to promote increased respect for children.

Our aim is to shed light on the Convention's instrumental function. We hope this chapter will also contribute to debate on the Convention.

1. Education

Children spend a considerable part of their existence at school. School, as a socialisation instrument, is therefore expected to be an adequate reflection of developments in society. The global social developments described in chapter 3 create new needs. Education has to take these new developments into account, or, at the very least, to be aware of them. In ideal circumstances, education can even provide the stimulus to such developments (the pro-active approach).

Developments in the concept of human rights go a long way towards explaining why the law is now a hot topic in education. Surveys and an increasing number of court rulings show that in many European countries pupils have taken to going to court to resolve disputes arising at school. This is a remarkable development, given that, in the past, education, traditionally based on absolute power to the teaching staff, remained for long time untouched by the law. A century ago, it would have been unthinkable for a pupil to appeal against the decision of a headmaster.

Although, because of the nature of the rights it confers, the Convention on the Rights of the Child in many cases imposes obligations on states parties, it also grants a number of general human rights to children. This new impetus to children's self-determination can not but produce new, important tasks for education.

Describing the relationship between education and the rights of the child is not easy. It is a relationship with many facets and problems, not always immediately obvious.

When a state ratifies the Convention, it imposes *three important tasks* on its schools. These are tasks existing side by side, but, which, given the comprehensive nature of the Convention are obviously interconnected.

1.1. The right *to* education

In various national and international legal instruments, the right to education is recognised as a universal fundamental right in society.

The right to education is already mentioned in article 26 of the Universal Declaration on Human Rights (1948), which, however, was not binding. Afterwards, it was repeatedly confirmed in binding international legal instruments. Article 13 of the International Covenant on Economic, Social and Cultural Rights, adopted by the UN in 1966, imposes an obligation on states parties to recognise the "right of every person to education". In its articles 4 and 5, the UNESCO Convention (1960) develops this right still further and deals more particularly with the principle of non-discrimination in education.

In the European region, this right became enforceable through the adoption of article 2 of the first Additional Protocol to the European Convention for the Protection of Human Rights and Fundamental Freedoms (1952).

The Convention on the Rights of the Child (1989) also reconfirms this right:

- Article 28 provides the means of enforcing it. The principle of non-discrimination, free access to education, the introduction of compulsory primary education are examples of subjects covered by this right to education.
- Article 29 contains detailed provisions concerning the aims and values involved: the development of the child's personality to its fullest potential, the preparation of the child for a responsible role in society, the development of respect for nature, mutual understanding and friendship among all peoples, and especially *the development of respect for human rights and fundamental freedoms.*

Both articles therefore impose the obligation on states parties to implement the Convention directly through their education policy.

At first sight, Belgium does seem to live up to the obligations imposed by the above-mentioned international instruments. Article 24 of the Constitution provides that "everyone has the right to education, *respecting fundamental rights and freedoms.*" Access to education is free for all children below compulsory school age (in 1983 the duration of compulsory schooling in Belgium was fixed at 12 years).

And yet a considerable number of problems to do with the right to education have arisen and the number of court cases is on the increase.

It would be impossible to deal with all these problem areas accurately in the confines of this book. We shall therefore limit ourselves to discussing a few specific problems, using the Belgian situation as a backdrop.

a. First of all, there is the strange phenomenon that the right to education (see article 24 of the Constitution) has, de facto, become compulsory education. Suffice it to refer to the opinion of the Belgian Council of State on the subject of the Law extending compulsory school age (1983). In its opinion, the Council of State points out a contradiction in the text, in that the point of reference is the right to basic education, as a right for young people, while from civil law provisions governing legal capacity and from the definition of compulsory schooling it can be deduced that this right can only be enforced through and vis à vis the young person's parents or guardians. In other words, the person who has to assert the minor's right is at one and the same time the person on whom the right has to be enforced.

b. Much doubt has also been expressed about the concept of "every person", which can be regarded either as a negative reference to the principle of non-discrimination, or as a positive reference to the democratisation role which can be played by education. Various studies have demonstrated the existence of inequality of educational opportunity for certain categories of people.
   Access to education may be free, but that is not the end of it. Free access means there are no school fees, but it does not mean there are no other (sometimes quite substantial) expenses for all kinds of compulsory or optional activities. These extra costs may well indirectly cause problems for certain people in asserting their right to education.
   Moreover there is a rather strange grants system (in itself an indirect recognition of the extra study expenses) in which the Mattheus effect plays an even greater part.
   Recent surveys have demonstrated that democratisation in education is stagnating. There are far fewer children from the so-called lower social classes in higher education and at university.
   Phenomena such as drop-outs, truancy, unsuitable curricula, etc. are all to do with the content and formal quality of education.
   All of this is directly connected to the real aim of education, which, in many ways, may be regarded as in conflict with article 29 of the Convention (i.e. "...the development of the child's personality, talents and mental and physical abilities to their fullest potential...").
   Finally, we should also point out the difficult situation of certain groups, such as immigrant and refugee children with regard to enforcing their right to education.

c. Expelling children subject to compulsory schooling, or refusing to enrol them is also a focus of highly topical debate. These are incidents which occur every year and have far-reaching consequences for children, who, at first sight, cannot fight these decisions. The growing number of court cases involving pupils/students and the education authorities clearly demonstrates that the former have very little protection and it is now clear that such cases are hardly few and far between.

1.2. Rights *in* education

The right to education, described above, is only one of many aspects which, taken together, make education an excellent yardstick against which to judge the rights of the child and their implementation. For instance, in many countries problems have surfaced concerning access to education or exclusion from it. These problems stem directly from children's problematic legal position within the education system.

We shall now examine a number of examples emblematic of the whole debate. We can, for instance, refer to article 3 of the ECHR ("No one shall be subjected to torture or to inhuman or degrading treatment or punishment") which has already been used to ban corporal punishment in schools (Warwick ruling, 1986). This example is directly connected to the rules on discipline, the debate on the status of punishment. In a later ruling, the European Court for Human Rights even cited article 28 of the Convention on the Rights of the Child with respect to corporal punishment at a British public school (Ruling Costello-Roberts, 1993).

In practice a number of legal problems also crop up to do with the examination system and the position of children. In other words, one of the first tasks for states parties, flowing from the Convention, will be to clarify children's legal position in education, to prevent breaches of children's rights (the defensive approach). It is in fact only natural that schools themselves respect human rights.

But there is more, much more. In its articles 12 to 16 the 1989 Convention contains important fundamental freedoms (the right to freedom of opinion, the right to be heard, the right to freedom of expression, the right to freedom of association and freedom of assembly, etc.).

All of this clearly implies the introduction of rights to self-determination for children, which must also be implemented in practical education. These are clearly *human rights in education*. We feel that far too little thinking has been done on this subject and that, in other words, work (i.e. respect for children) has yet to begin. To illustrate this statement, let us quote article 12,2 of the Convention: "...For this purpose (i.e. to implement the right to freedom of opinion and to freedom of expression), the child shall in particular be provided the opportunity to be heard in any judicial and administrative proceedings affecting the child...".

This is a clear reference to participation.

1.3. Rights *through* education

The UNESCO-Convention (1960 - article 5), and the International Covenant on Economic, Social and Cultural Rights (1966 - article 13) clearly indicate that education in states parties must aim at promoting respect for human rights. This is also in line with the spirit of the UN Charter and the Universal Declaration of Human Rights (article 26, 2), in that familiarity with human rights is the best protection against infringements. This view was confirmed again at the UN World Conference on Human Rights (Vienna, 1993). In December 1994, the General Assembly declared 1995-2004 to be the *UN Decade for Human Rights Education.* A detailed plan of action was drawn up by the High Commissioner for Human Rights. Regrettably, there has been little or no reaction from the member states.

The Council of Europe Committee of Ministers has also adopted a recommendation (Recommendation R(85)7), in which it urges member states to give firm encouragement to education on human rights and its promotion and asks member states to draw its recommendation to the attention of everybody involved in education. The recommendation contains a large number of suggestions to this end.

It is perhaps not surprising that we should encounter the same idea in the Convention on the Rights of the Child (article 29,1.b). The Convention even goes a step further. Article 42 imposes the obligation on states parties to make the principles and provisions of the Convention widely known to adults and children alike. Moreover, article 44, 6 requests states parties to make the contents of the reports they have to submit on the situation of the rights of the child (see chapter 5), widely available to the public in their own countries.

It goes without saying that a permanent, large scale information campaign on the Convention and its content is essential if the Convention is to be implemented effectively.

It is equally obvious that education has a major responsibility in this respect. Spending an occasional hour or two on the subject of children's right in schools would obviously fall short of the obligations states parties have taken upon themselves. Essentially, there has to be a shift in fundamental attitudes on respect for children's rights. Theoretical teaching on the values of human rights and democracy serves very little purpose, if they are not also put into practice at the same time.

Apart from this shift in attitudes, we will need changes in existing school curricula. Respect for human rights can be taught not only in history lessons but through practically every subject. Teacher training will have to be adapted to this new task. There might also be specific training for (regional) "press and information officers" and the setting up of a specific information system. Finally, all kinds of educational aids could be designed (texts, audio-visual aids, educational games, exhibitions, etc.).

Up to the present we can hardly speak about an intentional and systematic children's rights education policy.

2. Welfare

Historically speaking, assistance for children has been defined increasingly in terms of child protection.

This special care for children was institutionalised less than a century ago. Their roots are to be found in the criminal law. A separate approach to minors in the criminal law gained world-wide acceptance partly through the ideas of Social Defence. A juvenile delinquency was no longer judged in isolation, but rather as an expression of a "situation of danger" in which the minor found him/herself, be it because of his/her own actions or for other reasons.

Therefore child protection began to concern itself with other (non delinquent) children too. The aim was no longer to punish but to re-educate. Since then, child welfare has mostly taken place against this "child save-mouvement"-background (see chapter 3).

Naturally the Convention is equally important when we consider how to approach juvenile delinquency as such. Society's invoking the concept of children's rights must inevitably lead us to address the question of whether a juvenile delinquent has a right to a clear response from society to his/her unacceptable behaviour. Can we continue to accept sentencing of juvenile delinquents without explanation of the choice of sentence, or worse still, the argument that the reaction (i.e. the sentence) is no more than a reflection of "the child's best interests"? Then there is the issue of due process. The main articles to be looked at in this context are articles 37 and 40. To a certain extent, these articles are a summary of two UN resolutions prepared and adopted by UN Conferences on the Prevention of Crime and Treatment of

Offenders: the "Standard minimum rules for the administration of Juvenile Justice" ("Beijing Rules" - Resolution 45/112), and "Rules for the Protection of Juveniles deprived of their liberty" (Resolution 45/113): In these, we find, inter alia, guarantees against inhuman punishment and arbitrary arrest, and provisions governing legal assistance, as well as other fundamental legal principles.

The Convention on the Rights of the Child is, then, also extremely relevant to the way children are dealt with by the criminal law. This aspect however, the criminal law side of child protection, will not be addressed in detail in this book.

2.1. Child welfare provision and the Convention on the Rights of the Child

The Convention on the Rights of the Child also contains a "new" challenge for child welfare providers. There is no doubt that the law as a means of conferring and gaining respect does play a part in the welfare process, and particularly in the relationships created within it.

Opinions do differ on the Convention's (legally) binding effect, which inevitably means a need for some degree of caution. Some people see the provisions of the Convention as purely pro-active. In other words they see them as minimum rules, to aspire to rather than to use as positive legal references in court in specific cases.

We shall now examine a number of provisions of the Convention which can play a major part in (the discussion on) child welfare. As in education, here too we can distinguish between rights *to* and *in* welfare. In this part on child welfare we shall however mainly use the comprehensive nature of the Convention as our point of reference.

The comprehensive nature of the Convention is an excellent reason for focusing our attention not just on those articles specific to child welfare but on the Convention as a whole.

And yet the provisions which specifically deal with the welfare of special categories of children are not uninteresting. For instance article 24 deals with health care: "States parties recognise the right of the child to the enjoyment of the highest attainable standard of health and to facilities for the treatment of illness and rehabilitation of health. States parties shall strive to ensure that no child is deprived of his or her right of access to such health care services". Although this may sound obvious to us in our developed countries, we should still ask ourselves whether this is a right all children can assert. There are a variety of deprived groups for whom access to health care poses problems even today. There are, too, a number of moral issues, especially for minors, e.g. birth control in general and abortion in particular. With this in mind, we should take a closer look at another provision of article 24: "to ensure that all segments of society, in particular parents and children, are informed, have access to education and are supported in the use of, basic knowledge of child health and nutrition ...". This clearly stresses the need for a pro-active approach.

We find other, similar "welfare" provisions in article 21 (adoption), article 22 (refugees) article 23 (care of the handicapped),...

2.2. Rights *to* welfare

However the Convention on the Rights of the Child is of interest to welfare providers in a number of other respects. Perhaps, in view of existing national legislation, we should first mention article 41: "Nothing in this Convention shall affect any provisions that are more conductive to the realisation of the rights of the child and that may be contained in a) the law of a state party, ...".

Article 27 ("the right of every child to a standard of living adequate for the child's physical, mental spiritual, moral and social development") is perhaps another incentive to (re)read national legislation on children.

In this context, it is worth having a look at what national welfare legislation has to offer, especially as institutionalised child protection so far, does not seem to have managed in practice to fulfil the legislators ambitions, i.e. to take child protection out of the sphere of criminal law, deinstitutionalise it, achieve general prevention, ...

2.3. Rights *in* welfare

The Convention also contains a number of references which may prove useful in shedding light on a number of welfare or child protection initiatives which have gone or are going wrong.

Prospects for a more structural approach to the debate on the position of children in society in general, and in social and welfare policy in particular, are also on offer.

The first aspect we shall deal with is the relationship between parents and children. The Convention strongly emphasises the importance of the home environment to children. This is shown by the role attributed to parents in helping their children to exercise their rights (article 5): "States parties shall respect the responsibilities, rights, and duties of parents (...) to provide, in a manner consistent with the evolving capacities of the child, appropriate direction and guidance in the exercise by the child of the rights recognised in the present Convention".

Article 27, 2 says that parents " ...have the primary responsibility to secure, within their abilities and financial capacities, the conditions of living necessary for the child's (physical, spiritual, intellectual, moral and social) development".

There is also article 18 which states that "both parents have common responsibilities for the upbringing and development of the child."

The fundamental role of parents is (of necessity) complementary to that of children themselves (see below). Welfare provision can play an important part in shaping the role played by parents. Indeed article 18,2 could be taken as saying so: "...states parties shall render appropriate assistance to parents (...) in the performance of their child-rearing responsibilities...".

Article 27, 3 goes on to state that: "states parties shall take all appropriate measures to assist parents ... to implement this right".

Support for families is something which comes up over and over again in various articles of the Convention. Thus article 9 contains a provision requesting states parties not to place children into care: "States parties shall ensure that a child shall not be separated from his or her parents against their will, except when competent authorities subject to judicial review determine, in accordance with applicable law and procedures, that such separation is necessary for the best interests of the child...".

To improve legal protection of children, placing children into care is only considered acceptable when expressly authorised by a magistrate.

Furthermore article 25 "recognises the right of a child who has been placed ...to a periodic review of the treatment provided to the child and all other circumstances relevant to his or her placement."

The Convention, of course, also focuses on the child (as distinct from other sometimes necessary third parties, such as parents, see above). Involvement of children in the welfare process has to be turned into real participation. This point of departure is particularly important when the interests of children and parents (regarding welfare) clash.

The Convention constitutes a first step in the direction of equality for parents and children (in case of conflict), in its articles 12, 13, 14 and 16.

Article 12 guarantees for "the child who is capable of forming his or her own view the right to express those views freely in all matters affecting the child, the views of the child being given due weight in accordance with the age and maturity of the child.". This article also contains provisions on the right of the child to be heard in all legal and administrative proceedings.

Article 9, containing a provision against the separation of children from their parents, formulates the guarantee we encountered in article 12, i.e.: "In any proceedings pursuant to paragraph 1 (separation of parents and children), all interested parties shall be given an opportunity to articipate in the proceedings and make their views known".

Article 13 refers to the right of the child to freedom of expression, to be guaranteed not only in the welfare process. Welfare bodies could actively help children with their "freedom to seek, receive and impart information...".

Article 14 deals with a delicate issue: the right of the child to freedom of thought, conscience and religion. In this context recent Flemish legislation on youth welfare recognises this right exclusively through parents. Dealing with all practical consequences of article 14 would take us too far. Suffice it to say it can be regarded as yet another demonstration of respect for children as fully-fledged participants in the welfare process.

We shall conclude this item by referring to article 16, providing for protection of children against breach of their privacy: "No child shall be subjected to arbitrary or unlawful interference with his or her privacy, family, home or correspondence, nor to unlawful attacks on his or her honour and reputation." This is clearly also a fundamental issue in the context of welfare.

3. Labour

3.1. The phenomenon of child labour

Before delving into the consequences of the Convention on the Rights of the Child for child labour, it is necessary to examine the phenomenon itself, because a number of obstacles stand in the way of our understanding it. First of all, we have no definition, nor even any clear picture of this phenomenon. Moreover there are many dimensions to child labour.

3.1.1. *Lack of a definition*

In general, labour law does not explicitly define the concepts either of labour or of child labour, nor do international legal instruments get us any further.

Social legislation generally defines labour as work carried out for a wage under the authority of another person.

However, it seems legitimate to ask whether, in this context, notions generally accepted in the labour world are an appropriate reference, given that children form no part of this world because of the ban on child labour.

On the sixtieth anniversary the International Labour Conference's adoption of the first convention on child labour (in industry, 1912) the then Director-General of ILO, Francis Blanchard wrote: "This is what child labour is: *not* teenagers working a few hours a week for pocket money; *not* youngsters who help out at home; *not* children living on farms who lend a helping hand; but children who, at an early age, lead the life of an adult, working long hours for a pittance in circumstances which can damage their health, and their physical and mental development, children who are often denied any opportunity of meaningful education and training, which might lead to a better future for them." Consequently, he feels we should not describe as child labour work carried out by the child which forms an integral part of the socialisation process and a means of transmitting skills.

Using this sort of definition, the international community sets itself two objectives: the *final objective* is total *eradication* of the phenomenon. *Improving* working children's *living and working conditions* is an *intermediate* objective, an attempt to protect them from work unsuitable to their age or carried out in unpleasant circumstances.

The brandnew ILO-Convention 182 (1999) on *the abolition of the worst forms of child labour,* which entered into force 19 November 2000, is a striking example of this attitude.

The potentially damaging nature of work carried out by children therefore appears to be a fundamental element of the discussion. This led to revision of Belgian legislation (see law of 1st February 1993). The explanatory memorandum accompanying the law states, inter alia, that in our society child labour can no longer be considered a direct consequence of poverty, but rather one of the problems afflicting an affluent consumer society. This has changed the nature of child labour, but not necessarily its harmful effect. The ban on child labour therefore remains the norm.

3.1.2. *Lack of a clear picture of the phenomenon*

It is undeniable that, partly because of the ban on child labour, we know very little about the phenomenon, and the picture we have of it may be distorted by extremes. Large-scale systematic research, already carried out in several countries, may contribute to revealing this important facet of present-day reality.

3.1.3. *Child labour as a multi-dimensional phenomenon*

In practice, improving children's living and working conditions remains a major aim in even highly-industrialised Western countries. The law still allows a number of exceptions to the general ban on child labour, thus making it possible to keep the phenomenon under control. One good reason for having legislation is that it can determine the conditions under which children may carry out certain kinds of work, in order to provide special protection for those children who do work. Protection may vary with age and the specific needs of the child, including the need for rest and time to play alongside the working time of the child. Protection should not only be cover the physical, mental and moral integrity of the child, but also its wage. Protecting the child from economic exploitation means ensuring it is paid a fair wage to spend as the child wishes. It also means employers must fulfil their obligations concerning wages, social security contributions and insurance.

Labour should however not be regarded exclusively as a harmful phenomenon. It is one of the most important ways in which the individual can make a positive contribution to society, thereby improving his self-image ("the need to be needed"). It is generally assumed children have a specific contribution to make in two ways.

A highly-industrialised society needs to invest in the know-how needed to keep functioning at the same level. Maintaining knowledge and skills is essential and must be regarded as an important contribution to society. Modern labour structures leave this largely to children. Therefore, even while children may be excluded from the labour process, they nevertheless make an important contribution. Those who are in favour of this approach say that time spent at school should not be regarded as preparation for the labour process, but as an integral part of it, adapted to children, and, in the interests of efficiency, also best left to them. If this is correct, one cannot help wondering whether children are sufficiently rewarded for this contribution, or whether they are perhaps exploited.

In the production process itself there are apparently still tasks which can best, or even, only be carried out by children. Arguments in favour of child labour, for instance in the carpet industry, put forward in developing countries are not exclusive to the less developed parts of the world. The use of children in advertising is justified in exactly the same way. It is here, and in similar areas, that present-day debate on child labour is focused. In this context, a number of questions remain unanswered. Are these tasks, requiring the physical presence of children and in which adults cannot take their place, strictly necessary for society? Is the fact that illegal forms of labour are tolerated during a given period sufficient reason to legalise these forms of labour in order to have a clear legal position? Are we weighing conflicting interests (children's welfare vs. economic interests)? Is it possible to organise these tasks in such a way that exploitation is avoided? Besides the right to protection, can children's right to self-organisation and to participation in decision making be given due weight in the debate?

It is strange that when we talk about children, the right to labour (an important human right) is never mentioned. At the very most, arguments for such a right are put forward off the record, and, oddly enough, by people involved in projects for street children, a surprising source for this sort of argument.

We often hear it said that taking part in a play or a video clip, a photo-session or a fashion show from time to time can be an enriching experience for a child. The Belgian National Labour Council, for instance, reasoned this way when arguing against going too far in trying to legislate against child labour, claiming that "the positive side of carrying out certain tasks would also be lost". Many twentieth century educationalists are of the opinion that child labour, as an element in children's full participation in society, can have important beneficial effects. But obviously, we cannot afford the risk of harmful effects, which in itself is sufficient reason for effective legislation on working conditions.

3.2. The Convention on the Rights of the Child and child labour: other issues

The Convention on the Rights of the Child may well become a major stimulus to the adoption of child labour legislation.

In the explanatory memorandum to the Belgian legislation, for instance, the Convention on the Rights of the Child is cited as one of the main reasons for a review of the legal framework for child labour. The resulting new child labour law is one of the very first pieces of Belgian legislation to be based on the Convention.

Apart from its legislative impact, there are other ways in which the Convention on the Rights of the Child may prove important for child labour. One of its main features is its pro-active nature, making the improvement of children's position an ongoing challenge, rather than merely a matter of setting standards.

The Convention's comprehensive nature is equally important. It covers all children and their living conditions. Specific aspects of children's lives are therefore dealt with not only on their merits, but also as viewed in the global context of children's position in society. Article 32, among others, is very important in this.

Article 32 states:
"1. States Parties recognise the right of the child to be protected from economic exploitation and from performing any work that is likely to be hazardous or to interfere with the child's education, or to be harmful to the child's health or physical, mental, spiritual, moral or social development.
2. States Parties shall take legislative, administrative, social and educational measures to ensure the implementation of this article. To this end, and having regard to the relevant provisions of other international instruments, States Parties shall in particular:
a) provide for a minimum age or minimum ages for admissions to employment;
b) provide for appropriate regulation of the hours and conditions of employment; and

c) provide for appropriate penalties or other sanctions to ensure the effective enforcement of this article."

This article reconfirms the main policy principles regarded by the international community as the main levers for eradicating child labour. However, unlike ILO-Convention nr. 138 (1973) or the European Social Charter (1961), it does not contain clear age criteria, and is therefore regarded as less binding in character. Neither does the International Convention on Economic, Social and Cultural Rights (1966) state any age limit in its article 10,3, but it calls on the convention states to do this in their national legislation. On the other hand, the Convention on the Rights of the Child can fulfil a canvassing function on this point by referring to these other international measures. The fact that it was adopted unanimously and had been almost universally ratified further strengthens this function.

Article 26 deals with recognition by states parties of the right of every child to social security, and the obligation on states parties to provide it in accordance with their national law. Given the ban on child labour, children do not acquire this right by virtue of their own labour. If children work because exceptions to the ban on child labour are permitted, does this entitle them to social security? Could children invoke this article of the Convention in support of a claim for social security?

Article 3 stipulates that in all actions concerning children the best interests of the child shall be a primary consideration. Is a ban on child labour in their best interests, if one accepts the premise that doing certain kinds of work can be beneficial? Is the type of exception to the ban on child labour determined by the interest of the child or by the needs of the economy and society? New Belgian child labour legislation prohibits any work by children, which might be harmful to the child's educational, intellectual or social development, endanger its physical, mental or moral integrity, or adversely affect any other aspect of its well-being. Does this guarantee that the best interests of the child will be a primary consideration? How do we reconcile this with the stipulation that a child may be kept away from school, where the activity requires it? Who is involved in determining the best interests of the child, and where are such decisions taken?

How much say will children have in such decisions? Will children be part of the advisory committee, to be set up pursuant to article 12 of the Belgian law?

The Belgian law contains a provision giving the civil servant in charge of the case the right to impose special conditions ensuring, among other things, that the child agrees to carry out the work, and that the opinion of the child is given proper consideration, taking into account its age and maturity. Does this go far enough to comply with the Convention? Can it be said that the primary consideration is the best interests of the child, if the wish of the child not to carry out certain kinds of works is disregarded?

Articles 13 and 15 of the Convention recognise the right of the child to freedom of opinion, of association and of peaceful assembly. Do these articles not provide children with ways of participating in optimising their working conditions? Is it conceivable that children should set up workers' associations? And does the fact that children have this right mean they have to exercise it and carry the burden alone?

Article 4 requires states parties to undertake all appropriate measures to implement the rights recognised in the Convention. Does this article, then, impose a degree of responsibility on the state? In view of children's weak position in society, is it reasonable to assume that the state will facilitate their participation?

Children's participation rights, defined by the Convention, are essentially what we could term 'civil rights'. They could enable children to play a constructive role in society. Indeed it is expected that they will, as demonstrated by a sentence in article 40 of the Convention. Article 40 deals with juvenile delinquents, and provides, among other things, for how they are dealt with, bearing in mind the need to convince the child that it is a good thing for it to play a part in society. Since working is one of the most constructive ways in which we can shape our own environment, the right to work could be considered an important participation right. Can we deduce from this that the Convention regards the constructive role children can play mainly as an abstract concept?

In this regard NAT's, as a self-organisation of working children (see chapter 2), is very striking. Their main concern is not about the abolition of child labour but rather on better working conditions and protection. Remarkable they don't refer to article 32 of the Convention which is about child labour, but on the contrary they invoke article 12 on participation. Therefore they argue to be recognised as fully fledged partners in the local, national and international debate on child labour.

In the context of child labour, article 31 of the Convention, dealing with the right to rest and leisure, is obviously also very important.

Can we regulate children's active participation in culture and the arts while banning child labour without infringing article 31? It goes without saying that, in such circumstances, the state clearly has a responsibility to the child to protect it from any form of exploitation or anything which may be prejudicial to any aspects of its welfare.

Finally, we must refer to article 42. Knowledge of the law is evidently essential to ensuring its effective implementation.

4. The media

Given the Convention's comprehensive nature, it is hardly surprising that a lot of attention is focused on the media's importance to children. The lengthy article 17 refers to this explicitly, but a look at other articles, particularly the ones stating the Convention's principles, leads us to a number of remarkable conclusions.

4.1. Information and participation

We know that article 12 recognises the right of the child to participation, and states particularly that the child has to be allowed to express its own views in all matters affecting it.

Article 13 pursues this right to freedom of expression: "...this right shall include freedom to seek, receive and impart information and ideas of all kinds, regardless of frontiers, either orally, in writing or in print, in the form of art, or through any other media of the child's choice."

The Convention clearly makes an inseparable link between the right to information, freedom of opinion, freedom of expression and participation. These rights cannot exist independently. This has far-reaching consequences. The widely held view that children have to be "kept ignorant" (because they are only children after all) will prove to be unfounded. Debate has, in fact, already started, even on delicate ethical matters, such as releasing the name of the father in the case of artificial insemination with donated sperm.

We should also take careful note of the final part of article 13,1 "...or through any other medium of the child's choice." A number of "known" media, such as oral communication, printed information, or "art", having been mentioned, this passage obliges society, on the one hand, to look for those media which come naturally to children, and, on the other hand, to show respect for their choice.

This sheds a new light on article 42 which provides for the state to make the principles and provisions of the Convention widely known, to adults and *children alike*. The same goes for article 44,6 concerning the requirement that reports be made widely available to the public.

4.2. Pro-active nature

The right to information is reconfirmed in article 17, dealing specifically with the media. Because of the importance of a number of its features, we shall quote article 17 in full:
"States parties recognise the important function performed by the mass media and shall ensure that the child has access to information and material from a diversity of national and international sources, especially those aimed at the promotion of his or her social, spiritual and moral well-being and physical and mental health. To this end, States Parties shall:
a) Encourage the mass media to disseminate information and material of social and cultural benefit to the child and in accordance with the spirit of article 29;
b) Encourage international co-operation in the production, exchange and dissemination of such information and material from a diversity of cultural, national and international sources;
c) Encourage the production and dissemination of children's books;
d) Encourage the mass media to have particular regard to the linguistic needs of the child who belongs to a minority group or who is indigenous;
e) Encourage the development of appropriate guidelines for the protection of the child from information and material injurious to his or her well-being bearing in mind the provisions of articles 13 and 18."

The general thrust of this article is that the media can play an extremely important role in disseminating information which contributes to promoting the child's well-being in the broadest sense. The state is set a number of more specific tasks, which, strangely enough, are described in extreme detail (e.g. to encourage the production and dissemination of children's books). We should note the emphasis on knowledge of and mutual understanding by different peoples, and the focus on the children's cultural background. This is not unique. The same note is struck on education (article 29).

Children count for next to nothing in the media either quantitatively or qualitatively. This article gives strong encouragement to those in charge to change this.

Used together with articles 12 and 13, it should lead to a marked improvement in quality: children should no longer be treated as passive consumers but as active participants.

Paragraph e of article 17 is curious. It sounds defensive and re-active. In fact the revised draft convention submitted by Poland on October 5th 1979 considers the relationship between children and the media purely in defensive terms in its article 9: "Parents, guardians, state organs and social organisations shall protect the child against any harmful influence that mass media, and in particular the radio, film, television, printed materials and exhibitions, on account of their contents, may exert on his mental and moral development".

As of 1981, however, and throughout the whole drafting process, efforts were made to generate a more positive, pro-active approach to the media. The result is that the more re-active attitude is only a (necessary) part of a more positive approach. The reference at the end of the text to article 18 is very important, in that it reiterates the principles of the primary responsibility of both parents for the education of the child, and of the state's duty to assist them in this task.

The tension between *protection* and *emancipation* of the child is clearly present in the interesting field of media-law. For example, article 22 of the EC Broadcasting Directive of 3rd October 1989, which contained a number of provisions on the protection of minors says: "the member-states take all appropriate measures to make sure that no television broadcastings will occur that can seriously affect the physical, spiritual or moral development of minors". For a more emancipative view on children and media, there can be refered to the *Children's Television Charter* from March 1995, approved by the first *World Summit on Television and Children*, that, following article 17 of the Convention on the Rights of the Child, prescribes that children have the right to programmes of high quality, made specialy for them. Furthermore, the Charter mentions that therefore adequate budgets must be available.

4.3. Cultural rights for children too

Article 17 cannot be read independently of the extremely specific provisions in article 31.
"1. States Parties recognise the right of the child to rest and leisure, to engage in play and recreational activities appropriate to the age of the child and to participate freely in cultural life and the arts.
2. States Parties shall respect and promote the right of the child to fully participate in cultural and artistic life and shall encourage the provision of appropriate and equal opportunities for cultural, artistic, recreational and leisure activity."

This article confirms the right of children, indeed of any person, to participate in cultural and artistic life, as stated in article 15 of the 1966 International Covenant on Economic, Social and Cultural Rights.

To this the Convention on the Rights of the Child adds one of its most specific rights, the right to rest and leisure, to engage in play and recreational activities appropriate to the age of the child.

Chapter 7

CHILDREN'S RIGHTS IN THE EUROPEAN REGION

As we have explained before, there are many reasons why attention is now increasingly focused on children's rights world-wide. We have already described two fundamental developments: on the one hand, our *child-image* which has been undergoing change over the last decade and, on the other, the development of a more global *human rights project* since World War Two. It is clear that these two trends have stimulated interest in children's rights in the European region.

Through, among other things, regionalisation (i.e. dealing with human rights issues in culturally more homogeneous areas) it became possible to turn the ideals and moral obligations of the Universal Declaration into legally binding texts. The human rights project began to play a central role in Europe through the European Convention on the Protection of Human Rights and Fundamental Freedoms (ECHR), adopted in 1950 by the Council of Europe. We have already explained that the rights enshrined in the ECHR belong to the first generation of human rights, and are directly applicable in the 41 member states of the Council of Europe. The Universal Declaration was also "regionalised" in North and South America (Pact of San Josie - 1978) and in Africa (African Charter on Human and People's rights - 1986).

The second generation of human rights – economic, social and cultural rights – was enshrined in law in the member states of the Council of Europe through the European Social Charter (1961 revised in 1996). This provides, inter alia, for the state to play an active role in turning the rights contained in the charter into binding legislation.

While this process may reflect the above-mentioned changes in child-image, it is not always clear exactly what the role of the child is in the process of regionalisation of international human rights. In these instruments frequent mention is made of the status of the child, though the references are scattered over many different pieces of international, regional and bilateral legislation. It is not really possible to speak of a cohesive view.

In this chapter, we shall take a closer look at the position of the child in European society. The fundamental tension between *separate children's rights* and *general human rights* will once again be our back-drop.

First we must briefly examine the most important European institutions.

1. The distribution of powers in Europe

The word Europe means different things to different people. In this text, we shall look only at the two best-known organisations: the Council of Europe and the European Union (former European Communities). There exist about 24 organisations in Europe. Of course, some of them have consequences for children. For example we don't treat here the Organization for Safety and Co-operation in Europe (O.S.C.E.), the former Conference for Safety and Co-operation in Europe (C.S.C.E., cfr. Final Agreement of Helsinki 1975 and the Document of the Copenhagen Meeting 1990, Budapest Summit Declaration 5-6 December 1994). In the O.S.C.E.-framework very important consequences for human/children's rights can be seen.

1.1. The Council of Europe

The Council of Europe, like the UN, is an intergovernmental political organisation, established in 1949 to promote unity among its members through economic, social, cultural, scientific and administrative co-operation. At the moment, the Council of Europe has 41 member states, among them several former Eastern Block countries. The Council of Europe has its permanent headquarters in Strasbourg. Its two main bodies are the Committee of Ministers and the Parliamentary Assembly.

The *Committee of Ministers* is the Council's most important body as far as decision-making is concerned. It is made up of the Foreign Secretaries of member states, who meet twice a year, in May and November. Its powers, however, are limited. The Committee cannot take binding decisions. It makes recommendations to the governments of the member states and approves conventions, which are binding only on those member states which ratify them. The Committee is assisted by a number of committees of national experts.

The *Parliamentary Assembly* is composed of Members of Parliament from the individual member states. Each country is assigned a number of seats in proportion to its population.

Although the Parliamentary Assembly can debate all aspects of European co-operation, its remit is purely consultative. The Assembly makes recommendations (requiring a two thirds majority) to the Committee of Ministers which decides. It can also formulate resolutions (requiring only a simple majority) which it draws to the attention of appropriate bodies. It has more than fifty committees and subcommittees.

Not being a supra-national organisation, the Council of Europe's powers are rather limited. Its authority is based on the acceptance of its decisions by individual member states. Its annual budget is also limited. Its moral standing is high, though, especially on human rights. We have already mentioned the commendable work it did on drafting the European Convention on Human Rights (1950) and the European Charter (1961-1996).

The Council of Europe has set up a specially created body to monitor the ECHR: the *European Court of Human Rights*. Implementation of the European Social Charter is monitored through the *Committee of Independent Experts*.

1.2. The European Union

In contrast to the Council of Europe, which is an International Governmental Organization, the EU is a supra-national political body.

Since the Schumann Plan (1950), which was the inspiration for a *United Europe*, the European Coal and Steel Community (set up in 1951), the European Economic Community (EEC, set up in 1957) and the European Atomic Energy Community (Euratom, set up in 1957) joined together to form the European Community, which became the collective name for these separate communities, which were united by the Treaty of Rome in 1957. After the entry into force of the Maastricht Treaty, on November 1st 1993, the name changed to European Union (EU). This EU-Treaty was complemented by the Treaty of Amsterdam (1997) which entered into force May 1 st 1999). At the moment the EU has fifteen member states.

In the context of this book, we must pay special attention to the EEC. The Treaty of Rome, setting up the EEC, was signed in 1957 and amended through the Single European Act in 1986. The main objective of the Treaty of Rome is to bring about *European co-operation* in order to create prosperity, maintain peace and bring about political unity. The means to be used are mainly *economic* in nature, i.e. the establishment of a common market for goods, services, capital and labour. Economic growth would thereby be stimulated and the economies of the member states interconnected.

We all know how difficult the establishment of the internal market has proved. The Single European Act, as a complement to the Treaty of Rome, was designed to make EEC decision-making more effective and to introduce new areas of co-operation, such as environmental protection, improvement of working conditions, consumer protection and research and development (R&D). Greater emphasis was also to be given to the problems of weaker population groups and to the less-favoured regions of member states.

The Treaty of Maastricht (1992) and the Treaty of Amsterdam (1997) did not essentially change the basic objectives or the main economic means. This characteristic is of great importance to our subject.

The EU has four main institutions, established by the treaty of Rome: the Council of Ministers, the European Commission, the European Parliament and the Court of Justice.

The *Council of Ministers* is the legislative and decision-making body. It is made up of one minister from each member state. Which minister attends the council meeting depends on the topic under review. Education councils will, for instance be attended by the Education Minister of each country. In alphabetical order, each member state chairs the Council for a period of six months. Meeting of Heads of State and Government are also held. They are known as *European Councils*. The Council of Ministers is assisted by a Committee of Permanent Representatives, which prepares the debates in Council. The Permanent Representatives are the ambassadors of the member states to the EU. They are assisted in turn by working parties, made up of national experts.

The *European Commission* is the executive body. It has the exclusive right of drafting legislative and other proposals, and of implementing the Council's decisions. It has 20 members, appointed by member states for a 5 year term. Each commissioner has his own portfolio. The Commission is headed by a President. At the moment this is Romano Prodi. The Commission has its headquarters in Brussels. The Commission secretariat is subdivided into 24 Directorates General. Depending on the subject matter, the Commission brings in specialised organisations, such as ERASMUS/SOCRATES (an exchange programme for students and teachers in the EU) or HELIOS (a programme dealing with the handicapped). It also receives advice from all kinds of networks and experts, who carry out research on its behalf. Finally, the Commission is assisted in preparing and implementing legislative work by a large number of expert committees.

The *European Parliament* monitors the work of the European Commission and must be consulted on European legislation. Every five years the Members of the European parliament are directly elected in national elections. At the moment the EP has 626 Members. The EP plenary sessions are held in Strasbourg and committee meetings mostly in Brussels. The EP has its secretariat in Luxembourg. The Treaty of Maastricht and the Treaty of Amsterdam increased the powers of the EP somewhat, and it is to be expected that the powers of the European Parliament (at the moment very limited) will be extended in the near future.

The *Court of Justice*, established in Luxembourg, is the supreme judicial authority in the EU. Breaches of Community legislation can be taken directly to the Court only in very specific circumstances. There are also two indirect ways in which cases can be taken to the Court: when all national remedies have been exhausted and when breaches of EU legislation are reported to the European Commission, which can then refer them to the Court. The rulings of the Court are binding for all member states.

Finally there is the *Economic and Social Committee* (ECOSOC), which has to give an opinion on almost all Commission proposals. It is made up of representatives of industry, trade unions, consumers, environmental organisations, agricultural organisations, etc.

Unlike the Council of Europe, the EU is a *supra-national* organisation and its decisions are legally binding on member states. Community legislation is directly applicable, and therefore takes precedence over national legislation. In accordance with the EEC Treaty, the Council and Commission issue "Regulations", "Directives", "Resolutions" and make "Recommendations" or "Judgements". Only the "Recommendations" and "Judgements" are not binding. All the decisions have to be adopted unanimously.

The EU, therefore has considerable legal authority and, contrary to the Council of Europe, also an enormous budget. There is however a so-called "democratic deficit", in that the European Parliament, though directly elected, has very little say in EU legislation.

The EU has achieved very few of its social ambitions, which have had to take second place to its economic objectives, i.e. economic integration (the common market) and monetary integration, as described in the EEC Treaty. Calls for social and political union began to be voiced as ambitions only towards the end of the eighties (1989 - European Social Charter on Workers' Rights). However the Maastricht

Treaty (1992) has demonstrated that political rather than social union is the priority. Thus social policy is left mainly to member states.

After 15 months of negotiation in the Intergovernmental Conference (IGC, 29 March, 1996) the Treaty of Amsterdam was adopted on 17 June 1997. Although for the first time children are mentioned in this treaty (cf. infra), it does nog change basicly the aims and strategies of the EU. This means that at present the citizens of the EU are considered first and foremost as employees, employers, consumers etc... In this context children are not primarly children, but children of working parents.

Until the Treaties give the EU more power in the social field, we shall continue to have a two speed Europe: an economic then a social Europe. Developments in this second Europe are so slow that the social deficit just goes on growing.

2. Children's rights in Europe

2.1. The UN Convention on the Rights of the Child

All fifteen EU member states have ratified the UN Convention on the Rights of the Child (1989), as have all the member states of the Council of Europe. In other words most of Europe has now undertaken the obligation of implementing the Convention. This makes it the *most powerful children's rights instrument in Europe.*

As a consequence by its comprehensiveness and its legally binding character Europe, via its individual member states, is challenged to implement a *euro-political social contract.*

2.2. The Council of Europe

In addition to this new task, which is made compulsory by the UN Convention, the social position of children has in recent decades been under much more probing discussion at the level of the 41 Council of Europe member states. In this debate, the influence of our changing child-image and of the human rights project can clearly be seen. First of all, more and more often the European Convention on Human Rights is applied to children. Moreover, over the last few years, a number of unusual initiatives have been taken which are directly linked to children's rights in general. Finally there are a whole series of conventions, recommendations and resolutions dealing with traditional protection rights as they are to be applied either in special situations or to special categories of children. We shall now briefly examine these three developments.

2.2.1. *The ECHR: the child is also a human being!*

2.2.1.1. Direct and indirect reference to children

In the European region the ECHR is the fundamental human rights instrument, especially as regards civil and political rights (see above). However the ECHR refers to children only in two of its articles, although interpretation (in the courts) has brought to light a number of indirect references.

There is *direct* mention of the minor in article 5 on deprivation of liberty and in article 6,1 on the special protection to be afforded children at court cases heard in public. *Indirectly* article 8,1, on the right to respect for privacy (the independent right to a family life) and article 8,2, on the protection of this right, may be regarded as applicable to children. Article 2 of the First Additional Protocol, on the right to education, also refers to children of course.

2.2.1.2. Does the child have human rights?

However, apart from these direct and indirect references, the fundamental question remains whether the child has the rights stated in the ECHR (Is the child a person? Does it have general human rights?).

Article 1 states that "everybody" has human rights. Legal doctrine, as well as the jurisdiction by the former Commission and Court of Human Rights are increasingly confirming the principle that children should also be acknowledged as possessing these rights.

Article 14, on *non-discrimination*, is also important. Age is not specifically mentioned among the criteria for non-discrimination. Nevertheless, article 14 mentions "*other status*", under which "age" and "minority" can be understood. If the Court were ever to use this in that sense, which has not been the case up to now, the fundamental question for children – whether they have general human rights – would be solved.

2.2.1.3. Are children legally competent?

The acknowledgement of children as full legal persons involves not only the acknowledgement that they have rights, but also, and more especially, that they are considered capable of implementing these rights themselves. This brings us to the question of competence.

This draft was approved by the Committee in November 1994 and later (June 1995) by the Committee on Legal Cooperation. The latter then submitted the same draft convention to the Council of Ministers, which in its turn approved the text. What's more, the Council of Ministers also decided to make the draft convention available for signature and ratification as from January 1996.

This brand new European convention does not deal with substantive rights, but with the provision of *procedural rights*. By creating and, more particularly, strengthening procedural rights, which can be exercised by the children themselves, this convention promotes the implementation of the essential rights of children, especially in any *family law procedures* that may concern them (in fact the point of application is article 4 of the UN Convention, which provides for the use by the member states of all legal, administrative and other means to implement the acknowledged rights).

Although the area to which actual implementation is applied (family law) is relatively limited compared to the promising possibilities created by Recommendation no. 1121, according to some people this Convention still signifies a major step forward with regard to children's increasing capacity to act. In my opinion this is not the case at all. Article 12 of the UN Convention *acknowledges the right* of the child to make his/her views known and the right to the fact that account will be taken of this views in *every* matter of procedure concerning the child.

By contrast, this European Convention only offers the child the *possibility* ("... allow the child...", art. 6.b.), and as said above, only in a specific area of application.

In addition to this, closer analysis of the text shows (see section on supervision) that this Convention signifies a weakening of the UN Convention.

Considering the undermining effect it would have on the UN Convention, governments should be advised *not* to ratify it. The regionalization of the minimum standards of the UN Convention should aim to strengthen and not weaken the child's legal position.

If the Council of Europe is serious about this, it would be better for them to take up the idea of an additional protocol such as has already been proposed in Recommendation 1121.

2.2.3. *A mosaic of children's rights documents*

With the exception of this separate and extremely limited European Convention with regard to the exercise of children's rights, it is at the moment only the Ekman report and the ensuing Recommendation 1121 that provides a coherent view and approach to children's rights in Europe at the policy-making level. All too often ideas and powers are scattered over many documents and instruments, each dealing only with particular aspects and/or certain groups.

2.2.3.1. The European Social Charter

Besides the ECHR, the Council of Europe has another fundamental instrument: the 1961 European Social Charter, which entered into force in 1965 and deals with *economic, social and cultural rights*. The European Social Charter also refers directly (see, inter alia, article 7: the Right to Protection of Children and Young Persons; article 17: the Right of Mothers and Children to Social and Economic Protection; article 19.6 about the reunion of the family of a foreign worker) and indirectly to children. But it does not provide for any individual right to complain.

On 9th November 1995 an "Additional Protocol in the European Social Charter, including a system for collective complaints" was proposed for signature. The Collective Complaints procedure would reinforce the participation of management and work in NGO's.

On 4th April 1996 a revised European Social Charter was adopted by the Council of Ministers during the 662nd Meeting of Delegates (1-4 April 1996).

Monitoring in the form of obligatory regular reports by member states to a Committee of independent experts is required. It would be a good idea for NGO's to pay a little more attention to these national reports. It would also be useful if research institutes and universities were to analyse these reports from the point of view of children, in view of the fact that there is a considerable shortage of systematically compiled information on children in the European Region.

2.2.3.2. Particular conventions

Besides the fundamental human rights instruments we have already mentioned, a number of specific, sectoral conventions have also been adopted by the Committee of Ministers. We shall mention the most important of them. On 24th April 1967 a European Convention on *Adoption* was adopted. On 15th October 1975 a convention was signed on the legal status of *children born out of wedlock*. This gave such children the same legal status as those born within marriage. There is also a convention on the recognition and enforcement of decisions on *custody* of children (10th May 1980).

These three separate conventions together with the mentioned Convention on the excercise of children's rights (1996), each deal with the relationship between children and their families.

2.2.3.3. Sectoral recommendations and resolutions

The *Committee of Ministers* has adopted a whole series of recommendations and resolutions, each dealing with specific situations. We shall mention some of them, in chronological order:
- Resolution (72) 29, on the lowering of the age of full legal capacity.
- Resolution (77) 33, on the placement of children.
- Recommendation R (79) 3, on the integration of young people into the world of work.
- Recommendation R (79) 17, on the protection of children against ill-treatment.
- Recommendation R (84) 4, on parental responsibilities.
- Recommendation R (85) 4, on violence in the family.
- Recommendation R (87) 20, on social reactions to juvenile delinquency.
- Recommendation R (90) 2, regarding social measures resulting from violence in the family.
- Recommendation R (91) 11, concerning sexual exploitation, pornography and prostitution of and trafficking in, children and young adults.
- Recommendation R (93) 2, regarding the medical-social aspects of child abuse.
- Recommendation R (94) 14, on a coherent and integrated family policy.

The Parliamentary Assembly has adopted many other recommendations dealing with specific situations including, for example, the political participation of young people (Recommendation 1019 (1985)) the prohibition of child labour in commerce and other forms of exploitation of children (Recommendation 1065 (1987)), children's participation in family and social life (Recommendation R (98) 8), handicapped children (Resolution AP (84) 3), the abuse and neglect of children (Recommendation 1371 (1998)), human rights eduction (Recommendation 1346 (1997)), children's participation in family and social life (Recommendation R (98) 8),... Also a "draft" recommendation on "setting-up a European Ombudsman for Children" has been prepared (doc. 8552, 1, Oktober 1999).

It should be emphasized as well that, through some of its organisations, the Council of Europe also gives special attention to the child's rights to *information* and *participation*. For example, there are Recommendations on information and advice for children and ideas about participation in municipal and regional life.

2.2.3.4. Specific Committees

Particular attention must be paid to two specific actions taken by the Committee of Social, Health and Family Affairs. Firstly there is the so-called III.8. project. In 1992 the Council of Europe's Administrative Committee for Social Policy (CDPS) started up the *"Childhood Policies"* project (Project III.8). This project has produced a series of studies, recommendations and documents regarding various aspects of policy concerning children. The results were presented at a European Conference in Leipzig in 1996.

One extremely important fact is that this is a genuinely multi-discipline, inter-sector and *comprehensive* project. Secondly, and clearly influenced by the III.8 project, there is Parliamentary Recommendation 1286 concerning a *European Strategy for Children* (1996). The aim of the strategy is to make children's rights a political priority. It includes numerous proposals, such as a report on effects on children, an ombudsman, budgetary priorities, etc. The Council of Europe is to work on this with UNICEF. It is hoped that the Council of Ministers will already adopt this recommendation in 1997.

However on its Second Summit of Heads of State and Government of member states of the Council of Europe held in Strasbourg 10-11 October 1997 decided otherwise.

As a result of the Summit a new *"Programme for children"* was adopted by the Committee of Ministers. Only a weak link with the European strategy for children was kept. The programme very much aims at the child "protection prospective". Three key elements have been defined and identified: children and their environment, children and day care, and social support systems for children at risk of, or who have been victims of, abuse, violence and exploitation.

2.3. The European Union

First of all it must be said that all EU member states are also individually member states of the Council of Europe. Moreover, the EU as a community has also adopted the ECHR (Joint Declaration on Fundamental Rights, 5th April 1977). This means that its member states accept and comply with the ECHR. Everything we have said above (2.2.) on children is therefore also valid for the member states of the EU.

We have already mentioned the fact that all member states have also ratified the *UN Convention on the Rights of the Child.*

2.3.1. *Indirect attention to children*

The fundamental legal instruments of the EU (Treaty of Rome, Single Act and Maastricht Treaty, the Treaty of Amsterdam) do not set out a coherent child policy directly, although they implicitly allow for policy making: children's right as derived from the rights of their "working" parents.

There is also very little EU legislation (Regulations, Directives or Resolutions) which concerns children directly. Again policy-making is implicit rather than explicit.

Like other social policy areas, child policy is considered mainly an area of national concern.

And yet there is already an impressive catalogue of measures which concern children indirectly. It would take us too far to give an exhaustive list of them. There have been many scattered initiatives, mainly under pressure from the European Parliament, on: family policy, custody and legal kidnapping, migrants within the community, immigrants and refugees from outside the community (an issue also dealt with in the Dublin Agreement (1990) and the Executive Measures for the Schengen Agreement (1990)), poverty, education, child care, sexual exploitation of children, the media, the handicapped (Helios, Handynet, ...) the exchange of young people, minimum age for employment, working conditions for young people, toy safety, protection against accidents in the home (HELAS), youth unemployment, adoption, etc.

Within the European Commission, it is Directorate General V (DGV), responsible for Employment, Industrial Relations and Social Policy, which play the most important role in this area. However, the EU has no central focal point, a co-ordinating structure, for developing a coherent overall children's rights policy.

2.3.2. To a European Charter on the Rights of the Child?

The practical steps taken by the *European Parliament*, bring the various strands of the children's rights issue together, update and complement current texts, are of great symbolic value. Direct impetus was imparted to the European Parliament by the adoption of the UN Convention in 1989.

By 12th July 1990 the European Parliament had already adopted its first resolution on the Convention on the Rights of the Child, calling upon member states to ratify the Convention as a matter of urgency. The resolution also called upon the Commission to adapt the Convention to the specific situation in the EU, in the form of a draft European Charter on the Rights of the Child. On 13th December 1991 the Gröner Report on the problems of children in the EU was adopted and resulted in a draft European Convention, prepared by the Committee on Legal Affairs and Citizen's Rights. The Bandres-Molet report finally resulted in Resolution A3-0172/92 on a European Charter of the Rights of the Child (8th July 1992).

This draft charter does not, however, add very much to the UN Convention and even less to Council of Europe Recommendation 1121. It does look more closely at the specific situation in the EU, with special problems for citizens arising out of the common market and free movement of people (e.g. migration, social security, family reunification, etc.). It goes without saying that children are a particularly vulnerable section of the EU's population. Their specific problems however are mainly the result of the absence of a social policy in the EU. This is why the charter has mainly *symbolic value*: it is part of the wider European Parliament strategy designed to bring about a *social Europe*, a citizen's Europe, and therefore also a children's Europe. This also explains why there is no mention of a procedure for monitoring implementation of children's rights in the 8th July 1992 resolution.

We find a new attempt by the European Parliament to work out an active and coherent policy towards children in the Zimmerman report, which deals with measures for the protection of minors in the EU (1996).

There remains great scepticism with regard to this report and any ensuing resolution. The European parliament is not really a *law*maker.

In the new Treaty of the European Union, the Treaty of Amsterdam, a threesome of articles regarding children was adopted. In fact only "protection" of children was aimed at. For instance the new article K.1 tackling offences against children. Some other articles give limited compentence to promote children's rights: art. 13 enlarges the coverage of the anti-discrimination clause, amongst others to age; art. 137 on social exclusion can be used for children too; art. 143 on demography could be used to collect age disaggregated statistics which can improve the knowledge on children.

However "the child: a European citizen too" was not realised. Nevertheless a lot of basic ideas, and even technical solutions were prepared and suggested by NGO's.

These efforts are still going on at two levels: the drafting of the EU Charter of Fundamental rights and the new Intergovernmental Conference (IGC) to amend the EU Treaty.

The EU Charter on Fundamental Rights is likely to be finished by the end of 2000. Indeed in December 2000, the European Council in Nice (France) will take the decision about wether this EU Charter will become binding and be integrated into the Treaty or wether it will be just a (non-binding) declaration.

Euronet, a network of NGO's, already drafted a text to urge that children's rights are included in the Charter. The final decisions on the amendments to the EU Treaty via the process of the IGC will be taken at the same Nice Summit in December 2000.

Here again NGO's are active to influence the texts to include children in the basic treaty.

2.3.3. *ERASMUS/SOCRATES* - *European Observatory on Childhood*

a) Education

We are all aware of the importance for human rights of education, training and further training. The previous chapter dealt fully, and more specifically in connection with education, with the rules issued by the UN (c.q. UNESCO) and the Council of Europe.

The EU Member states are members of the UN and of the Council of Europe. They must therefore comply with these rules. A good way of doing this is provided by the *ERASMUS/SOCRATES* programme. The opportunities offered by this programme have already been explored. Since 1990 the University of Gent has been working on a specific programme on children's rights. At first this programme only involved *student exchanges*. Since 1994 this has been supplemented by the organization of an annual, intensive *"European Course on the Rights of the Child"*.

Both of them were co-ordinated by the Children's Rights Centre of the University of Gent.

b) Scientific Research

Quality education must be based on sound scientific knowledge. Unfortunately we have little knowledge of children for two reasons. They will be referred to again. First of all because there is no real *ethnography* on children. Children are in fact mostly looked at "in relation to" others (e.g. the family or working parents) and are rarely themselves the unit of observation (see chapter 2). This is certainly the case in the EU where they are regarded as "children of workers". In the second place, children are objects rather than *subjects* of research. They do not themselves participate in the acquisition of knowledge about them. We know almost nothing about how they interpret events, about their meaning-making. And yet there are excellent research institutes in Europe, which could contribute to filling this gap. Systematic acquisition and updating of knowledge on children would be an enormous contribution to the establishment and implementation of a European programme on Childhood policy. This is why we advocate establishment of a *European Observatory on Childhood* as a first important step.

3. Conclusion

The evolution of *child-image* and rapid development of the *human rights project* have not left the European Region untouched.

These striking macro-social dynamics are fundamental to the understanding of the evolution of the rights of the child. The speed of these dynamics enables us better to understand the confused, sometimes almost chaotic situation we currently find ourselves in.

In this chapter we have tried to establish some order in the diversity and multitude of rules, draft rules, jurisprudence, and institutions and organisations, with their different powers, in the region.

We have shown that the UN Convention on the Rights of the Child, ratified by all the members states of the Council of Europe, and therefore also by the EU, remains the main international instrument in Europe. A lot will depend, however, on the efficiency of monitoring (see chapter 5).

In this context, because of the ECHR and the promising Additional Protocol contained in Recommendation 1121, the Council of Europe will probably remain the most authoritative organisation for some time to come.

Results achieved in the EU level remain the most disappointing. The legal pursuant to the EEC Treaty, the Single Act and the Maastricht and Amsterdam Treaties simply do not create the circumstances in which a forceful social policy could be established. We can therefore not expect a real child policy in the near future. At the time Josie Mendes Bota, a member of the European Parliament, criticised the Community for spending twenty times more on each sheep than on each child (PE.148.896/def., 17th May 1991). Nothing has essentially changed.

Efforts by the European Parliament on children's rights therefore have to be regarded as mainly symbolic. It is only through ERASMUS, and the European Observatory on Childhood Policies, which we hope will be set up, that viable initiatives can be undertaken.

In practice, the efforts made, particularly by the European Parliament, in the field of the rights of the child, should be considered as mainly symbolic. Only the initiatives within the ERASMUS/SOCRATES programme and, let us hope, through the creation of a European Observatory on Childhood Policy, appear to constitute limited, but realistic objectives.

Anyhow, even if chances are meagre, still a lot is expected from the Intergovernmental Conference (IGC) of 2000 to include children in the basic treaties, which would give a legal basis to establish a real European childhood policy.

Also the drafting process of the mentioned EU Charter of Fundamental Rights sounds hopeful. Anyhow the debates during this process again is reflecting the basic issues: the changing childimage and the human rights project.

Perhaps the E.U. ought to make a substantial contribution to the consolidation of European social policy in general, and in the area of children's rights in particular, throught the authoritative Council of Europe. Otherwise, all this will remain the responsibility of the individual Member States, and hence an historic anachronism.

Epilogue

THE CONVENTION: AN ENDING AND A NEW BEGINNING

1. The ending

With its almost universal ratification, the Convention is in any case a major reward for the years of work done to summon up respect for the human dignity of children. We have selected below a few of the aspects of this reward.

First of all, from a *formal, legal point of view,* we must stress that from now on children's rights have a legally binding foundation valid world wide. The move from what was in itself an important moral code (Declaration - 1959) to a legally binding instrument (Convention - 1989) was indeed fundamental. It goes without saying that we should not ignore the remarks on the Convention's normative value (and its technical legal consequences) either. Yet we must put things into perspective where monitoring is concerned. It is not yet clear how reports are to be drawn up, by whom and containing what.

The *content* of the Convention (the substantive right) appears to reflect the two global trends described in chapter 3. The Convention is a culmination of these trends, because of the unique way in which they are blended together. The Convention is comprehensive and binding, and thus enhances the influence of the *human rights project.* Its implementation helps to highlight a new *child-image.*

We know the debate is not over. This was shown very clearly during the preparatory work for the Convention by the way the question of human rights versus children's rights kept cropping up. There are a number of remarkable achievements all the same. It is now recognised that children have a number of freedoms, such as the right to freedom of expression, to legal assistance, information, association and peaceful assembly, the right to freedom of opinion, conscience and religion,... All of this has enhanced the debate on self-determination.

2. A new beginning

Against the background of global changes, it goes without saying that at the very most the Convention can be considered a 'provisional ending'.

We have already said that the trends described are probably more powerful than we can now imagine. We shall limit ourselves once again to a few aspects.

One of the most important concepts implicit in the Convention is its *offensive approach*. The Convention refers several times to member states' obligation to promote children's rights. In other words, effective prevention of discrimination against children and therefore infringements of their rights, requires not only instruments banning such discrimination (defensive approach), but also instruments promoting these rights. The Convention should not only forcefully protect children against their continued social exclusion, but should at the same time bring them back into the life of society. The debate on participation which the Convention unavoidably set in motion is the perfect barometer of the efforts made to promote the human dignity of children. It is clear that education has an important duty here which it should not shirk. Spending only a day here and there on information about children's rights would be a caricature of this duty.

The need for a deliberate and systematic policy on Children's (Human) Rights-education is urgent and essential.

Obviously in the long run this offensive approach will contribute to a fundamental change in our *child-image*. "De l'amour vers le respect" Le Monde wrote in its headline the day after the adoption of the Convention, indicating immediately that there is no truth to the typical attitude in the *West*, that the "Convention is meant for the Third World", given that here all necessary provisions for children have already been introduced. Because of the development of the child-image into a much deeper pattern of values, generating more respect in our relationship with children will be a difficult but fundamental process which has only just started penetrating our social consciousness. We should not forget either that in our countries a lot still needs to be done to establish the rights of children in special categories or specific situations, e.g. third world children, migrant and refugee children, legal position of children under the civil and criminal law, and in social legislation, etc. Western countries will also have to keep using the Convention as a yardstick for what is happening in other countries, given the rapid process of internationalisation (of social and economic developments).

We feel the Convention is also a new and fresh instrument in the *North-South dialogue,* which seems stuck in a rut. Its substantive provisions repeatedly call for solidarity between children. Monitoring especially stresses the need for help, advice and mutual co-operation as a new opportunity to assist other states in their efforts to comply with their obligations to children. In their reports countries must also look within their own borders to establish whether they meet their obligations to third world countries in this respect.

The *duty to report* brings us to one of the most important challenges inherent in the Convention. We have called it the 'Achilles' heel' of the Convention. The *quality requirements* for the content (what is to be reported), the procedures to be followed and authorship of the report will have to be extremely demanding, because of the important function of the report (both nationally and internationally). The report will not only be a touch stone, it will be *the* means of keeping the Convention, and its raison d'être alive. We know the Convention exists not just to avoid (possible) infringements of children's rights (defensive or re-active approach), but also to generate (more) respect for children (offensive or pro-active approach).

Keep in mind that the overall human rights-project is hardly finishing its phase of *minimum-standardsetting*. The phases of *implementation* and *monitoring* have only just started. The human rights-project is like a baby just leaving maternity care! For sure this is the case of the Convention on the Rights of the Child.

Although last but not least, it should be emphasized that, because it is *legally binding, comprehensive* and *universally ratified,* the Convention is, historically speaking, a brand new and unique *geopolitical social contract* Few people are aware of this fact. Increasing awareness of it can make an effective contribution to a response to the monopoly of the free market and its unprecedentedly aggressive consequences, which is in itself new historically.

Appendix I

Declaration of Geneva (1924)

By the present Declaration of the Rights of the Child, commonly known as the 'Declaration of Geneva', men and women of all nations, recognising that mankind owes to the Child the best that it has to give, declare and accept it as their duty that, beyond and above all considerations of race, nationality or creed:

1. The child must be given the means requisite for its normal development, both materially and spiritually.
2. The child that is hungry must be fed; the child that is sick must be nursed; the child that is backward must be helped; the delinquent child must be reclaimed; and the orphan and the waif must be sheltered and succoured.
3. The child must be the first to receive relief in times of distress.
4. The child must be put in a position to earn in livelihood, and must be protected against every form of exploitation.
5. The child must be brought up in the consciousness that its talents must be devoted to the service of its fellow-men.

Appendix II

The United Nations Declaration on the Rights of the Child (1959)

Preamble

Whereas the peoples of the United Nations have, in the Charter, reaffirmed their faith in fundamental human rights, and in the dignity and worth of the human person, and have determined to promote social progress and better standards of life in larger freedom.

Whereas the United Nations has, in the Universal Declaration of Human Rights, proclaimed that everyone is entitled to all rights and freedoms set forth therein, without distinction of any kind, such as race, colour, sex, language, religion, political or other opinion, national or social origin, property, birth or other status.

Whereas the child, by reason of his physical and mental immaturity, needs special safeguards and care, including appropriate legal protection, before as well as after birth.

Whereas the need for such special safeguards has been stated in the Geneva Declaration of the Rights of the Child of 1924, and recognized in the Universal Declaration of Human Rights and in the statutes of specialized agencies and international organizations concerned with the welfare of children.

Whereas mankind owes to the child the best it has to give.

Now therefore, the General Assembly proclaims this Declarion of the Rights of the Child to the end that he may have a happy childhood and enjoy for his own good and for the good of society the rights and freedoms herein set forth, and calls upon parents, upon men and women as individuals and upon voluntary organizations, local authorities and national governments to recognize these rights and strive for their observance by legislative and other measures progressively taken in accordance with the following principles:

Principle 1:

The child shall enjoy all the rights set forth in this Declaration. All children, without any exception whatsoever, shall be entitled to these rights, without distinction or discrimination on account of race, colour, sex, language, religion, political or other opinion, national or social origin, property, birth or other status, whether of himself or of his family.

Principle 2:

The child shall enjoy special protection, and shall be given opportunities and facilities, by law and by other means, to enable him to develop physically, mentally, morally, spiritually and socially in a healthy and normal manner and in conditions of freedom and dignity. In the enactment of laws for this purpose the best interests of the child shall be the paramount consideration.

Principle 3:

The child shall be entitled from his birth to a name and a nationality.

Principle 4:

The child shall enjoy the benefits of social security. He shall be entitled to grow and develop in health: to this end special care and protection shall be provided both to him and to his mother, including adequate pre-natal and post-natal care. The child shall have the right to adequate nutrition, housing, recreation and medical services.

Principle 5:

The child who is physically, mentally or socially handicapped shall be given the special treatment, education and care required by his particular condition.

Principle 6:

The child, for the full and harmonious development of his personality, needs love and understanding. He shall, wherever possible, grow up in the care and under the responsibility of his parents, and in any case in an atmosphere of affection and of moral and material security: a child of tender years shall not, save in exceptional circumstances, be separated from his mother. Society and the public authorities shall have the duty to extend particular care to children without a family and to those without adequate means of support. Payment of state and other assistance toward the maintenance of children of large families is desirable.

Principle 7:

The child is entitled to receive education, which shall be free and compulsory, at least in the elementary stages. He shall be given an education which will promote his general culture, and enable him on a basis of equal opportunity to develop his abilities, his individual judgment, and his sense of moral and social responsibility, and to become a useful member of society.

The best interests of the child shall be the guiding principle of those responsible for his education and guidance: that responsibility lies in the first place with his parents.

The child shall have full opportunity for play and recreation, which should be directed towards the same purposes as education: society and the public authorities shall endeavour to promote the enjoyment of this right.

Principle 8:

The child shall in all circumstances be among the first to receive protection and relief.

Principle 9:

The child shall be protected against all forms of neglect, cruelty and exploitation. He shall not be the subject of traffic, in any form.

The child shall not be admitted to employment before an appropriate minimum age: he shall in no case be caused or permitted to engage in any occupation or employment which would prejudice his health or education, or interfere with his physical, mental or moral development.

Principle 10:

The child shall be protected from practices which may foster racial, religious and any other form of discrimination. He shall, be brought up in a spirit of understanding, tolerance, friendship among peoples, peace and universal brotherhood and in full consciousness that his energy and talents should be devoted to the service of his fellow men.

Appendix III

The Convention on the Rights of the Child

Adopted by the General Assembly of the United Nations on 20 Novembre 1989

Text

PREAMBLE

The States Parties to the present Convention,

Considering that in accordance with the principles proclaimed in the Charter of the United Nations, recognition of the inherent dignity and of the equal and inalienable rights of all members of the human family is the foundation of freedom, justice and peace in the world,

Bearing in mind that the peoples of the United Nations have, in the Charter, reaffirmed their faith in fundamental human rights and in the dignity and worth of the human person, and have determined to promote social progress and better standards of life in larger freedom,

Recognizing that the United Nations has, in the Universal Declaration of Human Rights and in the International Covenants on Human Rights, proclaimed and agreed that everyone is entitled to all the rights and freedoms set forth therein, without distinction of any kind, such as race, colour, sex, language, religion, political or other opinion, national or social origin, property, birth or other status,

Recalling that, in the Universal Declaration of Human Rights, the United Nations has proclaimed that childhood is entitled to special care and assistance,

Convinced that the family, as the fundamental group of society and the natural environment for the growth and well-being of all its members and particularly children, should be afforded the necessary protection and assistance so that it can fully assume its responsibilities within the community,

Recognizing that the child, for the full and harmonious development of his or her personality, should grow up in a family environment, in an atmosphere of happiness, love and understanding,

Considering that the child should be fully prepared to live an individual life in society, and brought up in the spirit of the ideals proclaimed in the Charter of the United Nations, and in particular in the spirit of peace, dignity, tolerance, freedom, equality and solidarity,

Bearing in mind that the need for extending particular care to the child has been stated in the Geneva Declaration on the Rights of the Child of 1924 and in the Declaration of the Rights of the Child adopted by the United Nations in 1959 and recognized in the Universal Declaration of Human Rights, in the International Covenant on Civil and Political Rights (in particular in articles 23 and 24), in the International Covenant

Unofficial summary of main provisions

PREAMBLE

The preamble: recalls the basic principles of the United Nations and specific provisions of certain relevant human rights treaties and proclamations; reaffirms the fact that children, because of their vulnerability, need special care and protection; and places special emphasis on the primary caring and protective responsibility of the family, the need for legal and other protection of the child before and after birth, the importance of respect for the cultural values of the child's community, and the vital role of international cooperation in achieving the realization of children's rights.

on Economic, Social and Cultural Rights (in particular in its article 10) and in the statutes and relevant instruments of specialized agencies and international organizations concerned with the welfare of children,

Bearing in mind that, as indicated in the Declaration of the Rights of the Child adopted by the General Assembly of the United Nations on 20 November 1959, "the child, by reason of his physical and mental immaturity, needs special safeguards and care, including appropriate legal protection, before as well as after birth",

Recalling the provisions of the Declaration on Social and Legal Principles relating to the Protection and Welfare of Children, with Special Reference to Foster Placement and Adoption Nationally and Internationally (General Assembly Resolution 41/85 of 3 December 1986); the United Nations Standard Minimum Rules for the Administration of Juvenile Justice (The Beijing Rules) (General Assembly Resolution 40/33 of 29 November 1985); and the Declaration on the Protection of Women and Children in Emergency and Armed Conflict (General Assembly Resolution 3318 (XXIX) of 14 December 1974),

Recognizing that in all countries in the world there are children living in exceptionally difficult conditions, and that such children need special consideration,

Taking due account of the importance of the traditions and cultural values of each people for the protection and harmonious development of the child,

Recognizing the importance of international cooperation for improving the living conditions of children in every country, in particular in the developing countries,

Have agreed as follows:

PART I

Article 1

Definition of a child

All persons under 18, unless majority is attained at an earlier age.

For the purposes of the present Convention a child means every human being below the age of 18 years unless, under the law applicable to the child, majority is attained earlier.

Article 2

Non-discrimination

The principle that all rights apply to all children without exception, and the States obligation to protect children from any form of discrimination.

1. The States Parties to the present Convention shall respect and ensure the rights set forth in this Convention to each child within their jurisdiction without discrimination of any kind, irrespective of the child's or his or her parents or legal guardians race, colour, sex, language, religion, political or other opinion, national, ethnic or social origin, property, disability, birth or other status.

2. States Parties shall take all appropriate measures to ensure that the child is protected against all forms of discrimination or punishment on the basis of the status, activities, expressed opinions, or beliefs of the child's parents, legal guardians, or family members.

Article 3

Best interests of the child

All measures directed at the child are to be based in particular on the latters best interests. The State is to provide adequate care when parents or others responsible fail to do so.

1. In all actions concerning children, whether undertaken by public or private social welfare institutions, courts of law, administrative authorities or legislative bodies, the best interests of the child shall be a primary consideration.

2. States Parties undertake to ensure the child such protection and care as is necessary for his or her wellbeing, taking into account the rights and duties of his or her parents, legal guardians, or other individuals legally responsible for him or her, and, to this end, shall take all appropriate legislative and administrative measures.

3. States Parties shall ensure that the institutions, services and facilities responsible for the care or protection of children shall conform with the standards established by competent authorities, particularly in the areas of safety, health, in the number and suitability of their staff as well as competent supervision.

Article 4

Implementation of rights

The States obligation to translate the rights in the Convention into reality.

States Parties shall undertake all appropriate legislative, administrative, and other measures, for the implementation of the rights recognized in this Convention. In regard to economic, social and cultural rights, States Parties shall undertake such measures to the maximum extent of their available resources and, where needed, within the framework of international co-operation.

Article 5

Parental guidance and the childs evolving capacities

The States duty to respect the rights and responsibilities of parents and the wider family to provide guidance appropriate to the child's evolving capacities.

States Parties shall respect the responsibilities, rights, and duties of parents or, where applicable, the members of the extended family or community as provided for by the local custom, legal guardians or other persons legally responsible for the child, to provide, in a manner consistent with the evolving capacities of the child, appropriate direction and guidance in the exercise by the child of the rights recognized in the present Convention.

Article 6

Survival and development

The inherent right to life, and the States obligation to ensure the child's survival and development.

1. States Parties recognize that every child has the inherent right to life.

2. States Parties shall ensure to the maximum extent possible the survival and development of the child.

Article 7

Name and nationality

The right to have a name from birth and to be granted a nationality.

1. The child shall be registered immediately after birth and shall have the right from birth to a name, the right to acquire a nationality, and, as far as possible, the right to know and be cared for by his or her parents.

2. States Parties shall ensure the implementation of these rights in accordance with their national law and their obligations under the relevant international instruments in this field, in particular where the child would otherwise be stateless.

Article 8

Preservation of identity

The States obligation to protect and, if necessary, re-establish the basic aspects of a childs identity (name, nationality and family ties).

1. States Parties undertake to respect the right of the child to preserve his or her identity, including nationality, name and family relations as recognized by law without unlawful interference.

2. Where a child is illegally deprived of some or all of the elements of his or her identity, States Parties shall provide appropriate assistance and protection, with a view to speedily re-establishing his or her identity.

Article 9

Separation from parents

The childs right to live with his/her parents unless this is deemed incompatible with his/her best interests; the right to maintain contact with both parents if separated from one or both; the duties of States in cases where such separation results from State action.

1. States Parties shall ensure that a child shall not be separated from his or her parents against their will, except when competent authorities subject to judicial review determine, in accordance with applicable law and procedures, that such separation is necessary for the best interests of the child. Such determination may be necessary in a particular case such as one involving abuse or neglect of the child by the parents, or one where the parents are living separately and a decision must be made as to the childs place of residence.

2. In any proceedings pursuant to paragraph 1, all interested parties shall be given an opportunity to participate in the proceedings and make their views known.

3. States Parties shall respect the right of the child who is separated from one or both parents to maintain personal relations and direct contact with both parents on a regular basis, except if it is contrary to the childs best interests.

4. Where such separation results from any action initiated by a State Party, such as the detention, imprisonment, exile, deportation or death (including death arising from any cause while the person is in the custody of the State) of one or both parents or of the child, that State Party shall, upon request,

provide the parents, the child or, if appropriate, another member of the family with the essential information concerning the whereabouts of the absent member(s) of the family unless the provision of the information would be detrimental to the well-being of the child. States Parties shall further ensure that the submission of such a request shall of itself entail no adverse consequences for the person(s) concerned.

Article 10

Family reunification

The right of children and their parents to leave any country and to enter their own in order to be reunited or to maintain the child-parent relationship.

1. In accordance with the obligation of States Parties under article 9, paragraph 1, applications by a child or his or her parents to enter or leave a State Party for the purpose of family reunification shall be dealt with by States Parties in a positive, humane and expeditious manner. States Parties shall further ensure that the submission of such a request shall entail no adverse consequences for the applicants and for the members of their family.

2. A child whose parents reside in different States shall have the right to maintain on a regular basis save in exceptional circumstances personal relations and direct contacts with both parents. Towards that end and in accordance with the obligation of States Parties under article 9, paragraph 1, States Parties shall respect the right of the child and his or her parents to leave any country, including their own, and to enter their own country. The right to leave any country shall be subject only to such restrictions as are prescribed by law and which are necessary to protect the national security, public order *(ordre public)*, public health or morals or the rights and freedoms of others and are consistent with the other rights recognized in the present Convention.

Article 11

Illicit transfer and non return

The States obligation to prevent and to remedy the kidnapping or retention of children abroad by a parent or third party.

1. States Parties shall take measures to combat the illicit transfer and non-return of children abroad.

2. To this end, States Parties shall promote the conclusion of bilateral or multilateral agreements or accession to existing agreements.

Article 12

The childs opinion

The childs right to express an opinion, and to have that opinion taken into account, in any matter or procedure affecting the child.

1. States Parties shall assure to the child who is capable of forming his or her own views the right to express those views freely in all matters affecting the child, the views of the child being given due weight in accordance with the age and maturity of the child.

2. For this purpose, the child shall in particular be provided the opportunity to be heard in any judicial and administrative proceedings affecting the child, either directly, or through a

representative or an appropriate body, in a manner consistent with the procedural rules of national law.

Article 13

Freedom of expression

The childs right to make known, by any means and anywhere, his/her feelings and views, unless this would violate the rights of others.

1. The child shall have the right to freedom of expression; this right shall include freedom to seek, receive and impart information and ideas of all kinds, regardless of frontiers, either orally, in writing or in print, in the form of art, or through any other media of the childs choice.

2. The exercise of this right may be subject to certain restrictions, but these shall only be such as are provided by law and are necessary:

(a) for respect of the rights or reputations of others; or

(b) for the protection of national security or of public order *(ordre public)*, or of public health or morals.

Article 14

Freedom of thought, conscience and religion

The childs right to freedom of thought, conscience and religion, subject to appropriate parental guidance and national law.

1. States Parties shall respect the right of the child to freedom of thought, conscience and religion.

2. States Parties shall respect the rights and duties of the parents and, when applicable, legal guardians, to provide direction to the child in the exercise of his or her right in a manner consistent with the evolving capacities of the child.

3. Freedom to manifest ones religion or beliefs may be subject only to such limitations as are prescribed by law and are necessary to protect public safety, order, health, or morals or the fundamental rights and freedoms of others.

Article 15

Freedom of association

The right of children to meet together and to join or set up associations, unless the fact of doing so violates the rights of others.

1. States Parties recognize the rights of the child to freedom of association and to freedom of peaceful assembly.

2. No restrictions may be placed on the exercise of these rights other than those imposed in conformity with the law and which are necessary in a democratic society in the interests of national security or public safety, public order *(ordre public)*, the protection of public health or morals or the protection of the rights and freedoms of others.

Article 16

Protection of privacy

The right to protection from interference with privacy, family, home and correspondence, and from libel/slander.

1. No child shall be subjected to arbitrary or unlawful interference with his or her privacy, family, home or correspondence, nor to unlawful attacks on his or her honour and reputation.

2. The child has the right to the protection of the law against such interference or attacks.

Article 17

Access to appropriate information

States Parties recognize the important function performed by the mass media and shall ensure that the child has access to information and material from a diversity of national and international sources, especially those aimed at the promotion of his or her social, spiritual and moral well-being and physical and mental health. To this end, States Parties shall:

(a) Encourage the mass media to disseminate information and material of social and cultural benefit to the child and in accordance with the spirit of article 29;

(b) Encourage international co-operation in the production, exchange and dissemination of such information and material from a diversity of cultural, national and international sources;

(c) Encourage the production and dissemination of childrens books;

(d) Encourage the mass media to have particular regard to the linguistic needs of the child who belongs to a minority group or who is indigenous;

(e) Encourage the development of appropriate guidelines for the protection of the child from information and material injurious to his or her well-being bearing in mind the provisions of articles 13 and 18.

Role of the media in disseminating information to children that is consistent with moral well-being and knowledge and understanding among peoples, and respects the childs cultural background. The State is to take measures to encourage this and to protect children from harmful materials.

Article 18

Parental responsibilities

1. States Parties shall use their best efforts to ensure recognition of the principle that both parents have common responsibilities for the upbringing and development of the child. Parents or, as the case may be, legal guardians, have the primary responsibility for the upbringing and development of the child. The best interests of the child will be their basic concern.

2. For the purpose of guaranteeing and promoting the rights set forth in this Convention, States Parties shall render appropriate assistance to parents and legal guardians in the performance of their child-rearing responsibilities and shall ensure the development of institutions, facilities and services for the care of children.

3. States Parties shall take all appropriate measures to ensure that children of working parents have the right to benefit from child care services and facilities for which they are eligible.

The principle that both parents have joint primary responsibility for bringing up their children, and that the State should support them in this task.

Article 19

Protection from abuse and neglect

1. States Parties shall take all appropriate legislative, administrative, social and educational measures to protect the child from all forms of physical or mental violence, injury or abuse, neglect

The States obligation to protect children from all forms of maltreatment perpetrated by parents or or negligent treatment, maltreatment or exploitation including sexual abuse, while in the care of parent(s), legal guardian(s) or any other person who has the care of the child.

2. Such protective measures should, as appropriate, include effective procedures for the establishment of social programmes to provide necessary support for the child and for those who have the care of the child, as well as for other forms of prevention and for identification, reporting, referral, investigation, treatment, and follow-up of instances of child maltreatment described heretofore, and, as appropriate, for judicial involvement.

others responsible for their care, and to undertake preventive and treatment programmes in this regard.

Article 20

1. A child temporarily or permanently deprived of his or her family environment, or in whose own best interests cannot be allowed to remain in that environment, shall be entitled to special protection and assistance provided by the State.

2. States Parties shall in accordance with their national laws ensure alternative care for such a child.

3. Such care could include, inter alia, foster placement, Kafala of Islamic law, adoption, or if necessary placement in suitable institutions for the care of children. When considering solutions, due regard shall be paid to the desirability of continuity in a child's upbringing and to the child's ethnic, religious, cultural and linguistic background.

Protection of children without families

The States obligation to provide special protection for children deprived of their family environment and to ensure that appropriate alternative family care or institutional placement is made available to them, taking into account the child's cultural background.

Article 21

States Parties which recognize and/or permit the system of adoption shall ensure that the best interests of the child shall be the paramount consideration and they shall:

(a) ensure that the adoption of a child is authorized only by competent authorities who determine, in accordance with applicable law and procedures and on the basis of all pertinent and reliable information, that the adoption is permissible in view of the child's status concerning parents, relatives and legal guardians and that, if required, the persons concerned have given their informed consent to the adoption on the basis of such counselling as may be necessary;

(b) recognize that intercountry adoption may be considered as an alternative means of childs care, if the child cannot be placed in a foster or an adoptive family or cannot in any suitable manner be cared for in the child's country of origin;

(c) ensure that the child concerned by intercountry adoption enjoys safeguards and standards equivalent to those existing in the case of national adoption;

Adoption

In countries where adoption is recognized and/or allowed, it shall only be carried out in the best interests of the child, with all necessary safeguards regarding the admissibility of this solution for a given child and authorization by the competent authorities.

(d) take all appropriate measures to ensure that, in intercountry adoption, the placement does not result in improper financial gain for those involved in it;

(e) promote, where appropriate, the objectives of this article by concluding bilateral or multilateral arrangements or agreements, and endeavour, within this framework, to ensure that the placement of the child in another country is carried out by competent authorities or organs.

Article 22

Refugee children

Special protection to be granted to children who are refugees or seeking refugee status, and the States obligation to cooperate with competent organizations providing such protection and assistance.

1. States Parties shall take appropriate measures to ensure that a child who is seeking refugee status or who is considered a refugee in accordance with applicable international or domestic law and procedures shall, whether unaccompanied or accompanied by his or her parents or by any other person, receive appropriate protection and humanitarian assistance in the enjoyment of applicable rights set forth in this Convention and in other international human rights or humanitarian instruments to which the said States are Parties.

2. For this purpose, States Parties shall provide, as they consider appropriate, cooperation in any efforts by the United Nations and other competent intergovernmental organizations or non-governmental organizations cooperating with the United Nations to protect and assist such a child and to trace the parents or other members of the family of any refugee child in order to obtain information necessary for reunification with his or her family. In cases where no parents or other members of the family can be found, the child shall be accorded the same protection as any other child permanently or temporarily deprived of his or her family environment for any reason, as set forth in the present Convention.

Article 23

Handicapped children

The right of handicapped children to special care, education and training designed to help them to achieve greatest possible self-reliance and to lead a full and active life in society.

1. States Parties recognize that a mentally or physically disabled child should enjoy a full and decent life, in conditions which ensure dignity, promote self-reliance, and facilitate the child's active participation in the community.

2. States Parties recognize the right of the disabled child to special care and shall encourage and ensure the extension, subject to available resources, to the eligible child and those responsible for his or her care, of assistance for which application is made and which is appropriate to the child's condition and to the circumstances of the parents or others caring for the child.

3. Recognizing the special needs of a disabled child, assistance extended in accordance with paragraph 2 shall be provided free of charge, whenever possible, taking into account the

financial resources of the parents or others caring for the child, and shall be designed to ensure that the disabled child has effective access to and receives education, training, health care services, rehabilitation services, preparation for employment and recreation opportunities in a manner conducive to the childs achieving the fullest possible social integration and individual development, including his or her cultural and spiritual development.

4. States Parties shall promote in the spirit of international co-operation the exchange of appropriate information in the field of preventive health care and of medical, psychological and functional treatment of disabled children, including dissemination of and access to information concerning methods of rehabilitation education and vocational services, with the aim of enabling States Parties to improve their capabilities and skills and to widen their experience in these areas. In this regard, particular account shall be taken of the needs of developing countries.

Article 24

1. States Parties recognize the right of the child to the enjoyment of the highest attainable standard of health and to facilities for the treatment of illness and rehabilitation of health. States Parties shall strive to ensure that no child is deprived of his or her right of access to such health care services.

2. States Parties shall pursue full implementation of this right and, in particular, shall take appropriate measures:

(a) to diminish infant and child mortality,

(b) to ensure the provision of necessary medical assistance and health care to all children with emphasis on the development of primary health care,

(c) to combat disease and malnutrition including within the framework of primary health care, through inter alia the application of readily available technology and through the provision of adequate nutritious foods and clean drinking water, taking into consideration the dangers and risks of environmental pollution,

(d) to ensure appropriate pre- and post-natal health care for mothers,

(e) to ensure that all segments of society, in particular parents and children, are informed, have access to education and are supported in the use of, basic knowledge of child health and nutrition, the advantages of breast-feeding, hygiene and environmental sanitation and the prevention of accidents,

(f) to develop preventive health care, guidance for parents, and family planning education and services.

Health and health services

The right of children to enjoy the highest level of health possible and to have access to health and medical services, with special emphasis on primary and preventive health care, public health education and the diminution of infant mortality. The States obligation to work towards the abolition of harmful traditional practices.

3. States Parties shall take all effective and appropriate measures with a view to abolishing traditional practices prejudicial to the health of children.

4. States Parties undertake to promote and encourage international co-operation with a view to achieving progressively the full realization of the right recognized in this article. In this regard, particular account shall be taken of the needs of developing countries.

Article 25

Periodic review of placement

States Parties recognize the right of a child who has been placed by the competent authorities for the purposes of care, protection, or treatment of his or her physical or mental health, to a periodic review of the treatment provided to the child and all other circumstances relevant to his or her placement.

The right of children placed by the State for reasons of care, protection or treatment to have all aspects of that placement evaluated regularly.

Article 26

Social security

1. States Parties shall recognize for every child the right to benefit from social security, including social insurance, and shall take the necessary measures to achieve the full realization of this right in accordance with their national law.

2. The benefits should, where appropriate, be granted taking into account the resources and the circumstances of the child and persons having responsibility for the maintenance of the child as well as any other consideration relevant to an application for benefits made by or on behalf of the child.

The right of children to benefit from social security.

Article 27

Standard of living

1. States Parties recognize the right of every child to a standard of living adequate for the child's physical, mental, spiritual, moral and social development.

2. The parent(s) or others responsible for the child have the primary responsibility to secure, within their abilities and financial capacities, the conditions of living necessary for the childs development.

3. States Parties in accordance with national conditions and within their means shall take appropriate measures to assist parents and others responsible for the child to implement this right and shall in case of need provide material assistance and support programmes, particularly with regard to nutrition, clothing and housing.

4. States Parties shall take all appropriate measures to secure the recovery of maintenance for the child from the parents or other persons having financial responsibility for the child, both within the State Party and from abroad. In particular, where

The right of children to benefit from an adequate standard of living, the primary responsibility of parents to provide this, and the States duty to ensure that this responsibility is first fulfillable and then fulfilled, where necessary through the recovery of maintenance.

the person having financial responsibility for the child lives in a State different from that of the child, States Parties shall promote the accession to international agreements or the conclusion of such agreements as well as the making of other appropriate arrangements.

Article 28

Education

The child's right to education, and the States duty to ensure that primary education at least is made free and compulsory. Administration of school discipline is to reflect the child's human dignity.

1. States Parties recognize the right of the child to education, and with a view to achieving this right progressively and on the basis of equal opportunity, they shall, in particular:

(a) make primary education compulsory and available free to all;

(b) encourage the development of different forms of secondary education, including general and vocational education, make them available and accessible to every child, and take appropriate measures such as the introduction of free education and offering financial assistance in case of need;

(c) make higher education accessible to all on the basis of capacity by every appropriate means;

(d) make educational and vocational information and guidance available and accessible to all children;

(e) take measures to encourage regular attendance at schools and the reduction of drop-out rates.

2. States Parties shall take all appropriate measures to ensure that school discipline is administered in a manner consistent with the child's human dignity and in conformity with the present Convention.

3. States Parties shall promote and encourage international co-operation in matters relating to education, in particular with a view to contributing to the elimination of ignorance and illiteracy throughout the world and facilitating access to scientific and technical knowledge and modern teaching methods. In this regard, particular account shall be taken of the needs of developing countries.

Article 29

Aims of education

The States recognition that education should be directed at developing the child's personality and talents, preparing the child for active life as an adult, fostering respect for basic human rights and developing respect for the child's own cultural and national values and those of others.

1. States Parties agree that the education of the child shall be directed to:

(a) the development of the childs personality, talents and mental and physical abilities to their fullest potential;

(b) the development of respect for human rights and fundamental freedoms, and for the principles enshrined in the Charter of the United Nations;

(c) the development of respect for the childs parents, his or her own cultural identity, language and values, for the national values of the country in which the child is living, the country from which he or she may originate, and for civilizations different from his or her own;

(d) the preparation of the child for responsible life in a free society, in the spirit of understanding, peace, tolerance, equality of sexes, and friendship among all peoples, ethnic, national and religious groups and persons of indigenous origin;

(e) the development of respect for the natural environment.

2. No part of this article or article 28 shall be construed so as to interfere with the liberty of individuals and bodies to establish and direct educational institutions, subject always to the observance of the principles set forth in paragraph 1 of this article and to the requirements that the education given in such institutions shall conform to such minimum standards as may be laid down by the State.

Article 30

Children of minorities or indigenous populations

The right of children of minority communities and indigenous populations to enjoy their own culture and to practice their own religion and language.

In those States in which ethnic, religious or linguistic minorities or persons of indigenous origin exist, a child belonging to such a minority or who is indigenous shall not be denied the right, in community with other members of his or her group, to enjoy his or her own culture, to profess and practice his or her own religion, or to use his or her own language.

Article 31

Leisure, recreation and cultural activities

The right of children to leisure, play and participation in cultural and artistic activities.

1. States Parties recognize the right of the child to rest and leisure, to engage in play and recreational activities appropriate to the age of the child and to participate freely in cultural life and the arts.

2. States Parties shall respect and promote the right of the child to fully participate in cultural and artistic life and shall encourage the provision of appropriate and equal opportunities for cultural, artistic, recreational and leisure activity.

Article 32

1. States Parties recognize the right of the child to be protected from economic exploitation and from performing any work that is likely to be hazardous or to interfere with the child's education, or to be harmful to the childs health or physical, mental, spiritual, moral or social development.

2. States Parties shall take legislative, administrative, social and educational measures to ensure the implementation of this article. To this end, and having regard to the relevant provi-

sions of other international instruments, States Parties shall in particular:

(a) provide for a minimum age or minimum ages for admissions to employment;

(b) provide for appropriate regulation of the hours and conditions of employment; and

(c) provide for appropriate penalties or other sanctions to ensure the effective enforcement of this article.

Article 33

Drug abuse

States Parties shall take all appropriate measures, including legislative, administrative, social and educational measures, to protect children from the illicit use of narcotic drugs and psychotropic substances as defined in the relevant international treaties, and to prevent the use of children in the illicit production and trafficking of such substances.

The child's right to protection from the use of narcotic and psychotropic drugs and from being involved in their production or distribution.

Article 34

Sexual exploitation

States Parties undertake to protect the child from all forms of sexual exploitation and sexual abuse. For these purposes States Parties shall in particular take all appropriate national, bilateral and multilateral measures to prevent:

(a) the inducement or coercion of a child to engage in any unlawful sexual activity;

(b) the exploitative use of children in prostitution or other unlawful sexual practices;

(c) the exploitative use of children in pornographic performances and materials.

The childs right to protection from sexual exploitation and abuse, including prostitution and involvement in pornography.

Article 35

Sale, trafficking and abduction

States Parties shall take all appropriate national, bilateral and multilateral measures to prevent the abduction, the sale of or traffic in children for any purpose or in any form.

The States obligation to make every effort to prevent the sale, trafficking and abduction of children.

Article 36

Other forms of exploitation

States Parties shall protect the child against all other forms of exploitation prejudicial to any aspects of the child's welfare.

The child's right to protection from all other forms of exploitation not covered in articles 32, 33, 34 and 35.

Article 37

States Parties shall ensure that:

(a) No child shall be subjected to torture or other cruel, inhuman or degrading treatment or punishment. Neither capital punishment nor life imprisonment without possibility of release shall be imposed for offences committed by persons below 18 years of age;

(b) No child shall be deprived of his or her liberty unlawfully or arbitrarily. The arrest, detention or imprisonment of a child shall be in conformity with the law and shall be used only as a measure of last resort and for the shortest appropriate period of time;

(c) Every child deprived of liberty shall be treated with humanity and respect for the inherent dignity of the human person, and in a manner which takes into account the needs of persons of their age. In particular every child deprived of liberty shall be separated from adults unless it is considered in the child's best interest not to do so and shall have the right to maintain contact with his or her family through correspondence and visits, save in exceptional circumstances;

(d) Every child deprived of his or her liberty shall have the right to prompt access to legal and other appropriate assistance as well as the right to challenge the legality of the deprivation of his or her liberty before a court or other competent, independent and impartial authority and to a prompt decision on any such action.

Torture and deprivation of liberty

The prohibition of torture, cruel treatment or punishment, capital punishment, life imprisonment, and unlawful arrest or deprivation of liberty. The principles of appropriate treatment, separation from detained adults, contact with family and access to legal and other assistance.

Article 38

1. States Parties undertake to respect and to ensure respect for rules of international humanitarian law applicable to them in armed conflicts which are relevant to the child.

2. States Parties shall take all feasible measures to ensure that persons who have not attained the age of 15 years do not take a direct part in hostilities.

3. States Parties shall refrain from recruiting any person who has not attained the age of 15 years into their armed forces. In recruiting among those persons who have attained the age of 15 years but who have not attained the age of 18 years, States Parties shall endeavour to give priority to those who are oldest.

4. In accordance with their obligations under international humanitarian law to protect the civilian population in armed conflicts, States Parties shall take all feasible measures to ensure protection and care of children who are affected by an armed conflict.

Armed conflicts

The principle that no child under 15 take a direct part in hostilities or be recruited into the armed forces, and that all children affected by armed conflict benefit from protection and care.

Article 39

Rehabilitative care

States Parties shall take all appropriate measures to promote physical and psychological recovery and social re-integration of a child victim of: any form of neglect, exploitation, or abuse; torture or any other form of cruel, inhuman or degrading treatment or punishment; or armed conflicts. Such recovery and re-integration shall take place in an environment which fosters the health, self-respect and dignity of the child.

The States obligation to ensure that child victims of armed conflicts, torture, neglect, maltreatment or exploitation receive appropriate treatment for their recovery and social re-integration.

Article 40

Administration of juvenile justice

1. States Parties recognize the right of every child alleged as, accused of, or recognized as having infringed the penal law to be treated in a manner consistent with the promotion of the child's sense of dignity and worth, which reinforces the child's respect for the human rights and fundamental freedoms of others and which takes into account the child's age and the desirability of promoting the child's re-integration and the child's assuming a constructive role in society.

2. To this end, and having regard to the relevant provisions of international instruments, States Parties shall, in particular, ensure that:

(a) No child shall be alleged as, be accused of, or recognized as having infringed the penal law by reason of acts or omissions which were not prohibited by national or international law at the time they were committed;

(b) Every child alleged as or accused of having infringed the penal law has at least the following guarantees:

(i) to be presumed innocent until proven guilty according to law;

(ii) to be informed promptly and directly of the charges against him or her, and if appropriate through his or her parents or legal guardian, and to have legal or other appropriate assistance in the preparation and presentation of his or her defence;

(iii) to have the matter determined without delay by a competent, independent and impartial authority or judicial body in a fair hearing according to law, in the presence of legal or other appropriate assistance and, unless it is considered not to be in the best interest of the child, in particular, taking into account his or her age or situation, his or her parents or legal guardians;

(iv) not to be compelled to give testimony or to confess guilt; to examine or have examined adverse witnesses and to obtain the participation and examination of witnesses on his or her behalf under conditions of equality;

The right of children alleged or recognized as having committed an offence to respect for their global human rights and, in particular, to benefit from all aspects of the due process of law, including legal or other assistance in preparing and presenting their defence. The principle that, wherever possible, recourse to judicial proceedings and institutional placements should be avoided.

(v) if considered to have infringed the penal law, to have this decision and any measures imposed in consequence thereof reviewed by a higher competent, independent and impartial authority or judicial body according to law;

(vi) to have the free assistance of an interpreter if the child cannot understand or speak the language used;

(vii) to have his or her privacy fully respected at all stages of the proceedings.

3. States Parties shall seek to promote the establishment of laws, procedures, authorities and institutions specifically applicable to children alleged as, accused of, or recognized as having infringed the penal law, and in particular:

(a) the establishment of a minimum age below which children shall be presumed not to have the capacity to infringe the penal law;

(b) whenever appropriate and desirable, measures for dealing with such children without resorting to judicial proceedings, providing that human rights and legal safeguards are fully respected.

4. A variety of dispositions, such as care, guidance and supervision orders; counselling; probation; foster care; education and vocational training programmes and other alternatives to institutional care shall be available to ensure that children are dealt with in a manner appropriate to their well-being and proportionate both to their circumstances and the offence.

Article 41

Nothing in this Convention shall affect any provisions that are more conducive to the realization of the rights of the child and that may be contained in:

(a) the law of a State Party; or

(b) international law in force for that State.

Respect for existing standards

The principle that, if any standards set in national law or other applicable international instruments are higher than those of this Convention, it is the higher standard that applies.

PART II

Article 42

States Parties undertake to make the principles and provisions of the Convention widely known, by appropriate and active means, to adults and children alike.

Implementation and entry into force

The provisions of articles 42 - 54 notably foresee:

Article 43

1. For the purpose of examining the progress made by States Parties in achieving the realization of the obligations undertaken in the present Convention, there shall be established a Committee on the Rights of the Child, which shall carry out the functions hereinafter provided.

2. The Committee shall consist of 10 experts of high moral standing and recognized competence in the field covered by this Convention. The members of the Committee shall be elected by States Parties from among their nationals and shall serve in their personal capacity, consideration being given to equitable geographical distribution as well as to the principal legal systems.

3. The members of the Committee shall be elected by secret ballot from a list of persons nominated by States Parties. Each State Party may nominate one person from among its own nationals.

4. The initial election to the Committee shall be held no later than six months after the date of the entry into force of the present Convention and thereafter every second year. At least four months before the date of each election, the Secretary-General of the United Nations shall address a letter to States Parties inviting them to submit their nominations within two months. The Secretary-General shall subsequently prepare a list in alphabetical order of all persons thus nominated, indicating States Parties which have nominated them, and shall submit it to the States Parties to the present Convention.

5. The elections shall be held at meetings of States Parties convened by the Secretary-General at United Nations Headquarters. At those meetings, for which two-thirds of States Parties shall constitute a quorum, the persons elected to the Committee shall be those who obtain the largest number of votes and an absolute majority of the votes of the representatives of States Parties present and voting.

6. The members of the Committee shall be elected for a term of four years. They shall be eligible for re-election if renominated. The term of five of the members elected at the first election shall expire at the end of two years; immediately after the first election the names of these five members shall be chosen by lot by the Chairman of the meeting.

7. If a member of the Committee dies or resigns or declares that for any other cause he or she can no longer perform the duties of the Committee, the State Party which nominated the member shall appoint another expert from among its nationals to serve for the remainder of the term, subject to the approval of the Committee.

8. The Committee shall establish its own rules of procedure.

(i) the States obligation to make the rights contained in this Convention widely known to both adults and children.

(ii) the setting up of a Committee on the Rights of the Child composed of ten experts, which will consider reports that States Parties to the Convention are to submit two years after ratification and every five years thereafter. The Convention enters into force – and the Committee would therefore be set up – once 20 countries have ratified it.

(iii) States Parties are to make their reports widely available to the general public.

(iv) The Committee may propose that special studies be undertaken on specific issues relating to the rights of the child, and may make its evaluations known to each State Party concerned as well as to the UN General Assembly.

(v) In order to foster the effective implementation of the Convention and to encourage international co-operation, the specialized agencies of the UN (such as the ILO, WHO and UNESCO) and UNICEF would be able to attend the meetings of the Committee. Together with any other body recognized as competent, including NGO's in consultative status with the UN and UN organs such as the UNHCR, they can submit pertinent information to the Committee and be asked to advise on the optimal implementation of the Convention.

9. The Committee shall elect its officers for a period of two years.

10. The meetings of the Committee shall normally be held at the United Nations Headquarters or at any other convenient place as determined by the Committee. The Committee shall normally meet annually. The duration of the meetings of the Committee shall be determined, and reviewed, if necessary, by a meeting of the States Parties to the present Convention, subject to the approval of the General Assembly.

11. The Secretary-General of the United Nations shall provide the necessary staff and facilities for the effective performance of the functions of the Committee under the present Convention.

12. With the approval of the General Assembly, the members of the Committee established under the present Convention shall receive emoluments from the United Nations resources on such terms and conditions as the Assembly may decide.

Article 44

1. States Parties undertake to submit to the Committee, through the Secretary-General of the United Nations, reports on the measures they have adopted which give effect to the rights recognized herein and on the progress made on the enjoyment of those rights:

(a) within two years of the entry into force of the Convention for the State Party concerned,

(b) thereafter every five years

2. Reports made under this article shall indicate factors and difficulties, if any, affecting the degree of fulfilment of the obligations under the present Convention. Reports shall also contain sufficient information to provide the Committee with a comprehensive understanding of the implementation of the Convention in the country concerned.

3. A State Party which has submitted a comprehensive initial report to the Committee need not in its subsequent reports submitted in accordance with paragraph 1(b) repeat basic information previously provided.

4. The Committee may request from States Parties further information relevant to the implementation of the Convention.

5. The Committee shall submit to the General Assembly of the United Nations through the Economic and Social Council, every two years, reports on its activities.

6. States Parties shall make their reports widely available to the public in their own countries.

Article 45

In order to foster the effective implementation of the Convention and to encourage international co-operation in the field covered by the Convention:

(a) The specialized agencies, UNICEF and other United Nations organs shall be entitled to be represented at the consideration of the implementation of such provisions of the present Convention as fall within the scope of their mandate. The Committee may invite the specialized agencies, UNICEF and other competent bodies as it may consider appropriate to provide expert advice on the implementation of the Convention in areas falling within the scope of their respective mandates. The Committee may invite the specialized agencies, UNICEF and other United Nations organs to submit reports on the implementation of the Convention in areas falling within the scope of their activities.

(b) The Committee shall transmit, as it may consider appropriate, to the specialized agencies, UNICEF and other competent bodies, any reports from States Parties that contain a request, or indicate a need, for technical advice or assistance along with the Committees observations and suggestions, if any, on these requests or indications.

(c) the Committee may recommend to the General Assembly to request the Secretary-General to undertake on its behalf studies on specific issues relating to the rights of the child.

(d) the Committee may make suggestions and general recommendations based on information received pursuant to articles 44 and 45 of this Convention. Such suggestions and general recommendations shall be transmitted to any State Party concerned and reported to the General Assembly, together with comments, if any, from States Parties.

PART III

Article 46

The present Convention shall be open for signature by all States.

Article 47

The present Convention is subject to ratification. Instruments of ratification shall be deposited with the Secretary-General of the United Nations.

Article 48

The present Convention shall remain open for accession by any State. The instruments of accession shall be deposited with the Secretary-General of the United Nations.

Article 49

1. The present Convention shall enter into force on the thirtieth day following the date of deposit with the Secretary-General of the United Nations of the twentieth instrument of ratification or accession.

2. For each State ratifying or acceding to the Convention after the deposit of the twentieth instrument of ratification or accession, the Convention shall enter into force on the thirtieth day after the deposit by such State of its instrument of ratification or accession.

Article 50

1. Any State Party may propose an amendment and file it with the Secretary-General of the United Nations. The Secretary-General shall thereupon communicate the proposed amendment to States Parties with a request that they indicate whether they favour a conference of States Parties for the purpose of considering and voting upon the proposals. In the event that within four months from the date of such communication at least one-third of the States Parties favour such a conference, the Secretary-General shall convene the conference under the auspices of the United Nations. Any amendment adopted by a majority of States Parties present and voting at the conference shall be submitted to the General Assembly of the United Nations for approval.

2. An amendment adopted in accordance with paragraph (1) of this article shall enter into force when it has been approved by the General Assembly of the United Nations and accepted by a two-thirds majority of States Parties.

3. When an amendment enters into force, it shall be binding on those States Parties which have accepted it, other States Parties still being bound by the provisions of this Convention and any earlier amendments which they have accepted.

Article 51

1. The Secretary-General of the United Nations shall receive and circulate to all States the text of reservations made by States at the time of ratification or accession.

2. A reservation incompatible with the object and purpose of the present Convention shall not be permitted.

3. Reservations may be withdrawn at any time by notification to this effect addressed to the Secretary-General of the United Nations who shall then inform all States. Such notification shall take effect on the date on which it is received by the Secretary-General.

Article 52

A State Party may denounce this Convention by written notification to the Secretary-General of the United Nations. Denunciation becomes effective one year after the date of receipt of the notification by the Secretary-General.

Article 53

The Secretary-General of the United Nations is designated as the depositary of the present Convention.

Article 54

The original of the present Convention, of which the Arabic, Chinese, English, French, Russian and Spanish texts are equally authentic, shall be deposited with the Secretary-General of the United Nations.

In witness thereof the undersigned plenipotentiaries, being duly authorized thereto by their respective governments, have signed the present Convention.

Appendix IV

Optional Protocol to the Convention on the Rights of the Child on the involvement of children in armed conflict

(Adopted by the General Assembly of the United Nations on 25 May 2000)

The States Parties to the present Protocol,

Encouraged by the overwhelming support for the Convention on the Rights of the Child, demonstrating the widespread commitment that exists to strive for the promotion and protection of the rights of the child,

Reaffirming that the rights of children require special protection, and calling for continuous improvement of the situation of children without distinction, as well as for their development and education in conditions of peace and security,

Disturbed by the harmful and widespread impact of armed conflict on children and the long-term consequences this has for durable peace, security and development,

Condemning the targeting of children in situations of armed conflict and direct attacks on objects protected under international law, including places generally having a significant presence of children, such as schools and hospitals.

Noting the adoption of the Statute of the International Criminal Court and, in particular, its inclusion as a war crime of conscripting or enlisting children under the age of 15 years or using them to participate actively in hostilities in both international and non-international armed conflicts,

Considering, therefore, that to strengthen further the implementation of rights recognized in the Convention on the Rights of the Child there is a need to increase the protection of children from involvement in armed conflict,

Noting that article 1 of the Convention on the Rights of the Child specifies that, for the purposes of that Convention, a child means every human being below the age of 18 years unless, under the law applicable to the child, majority is attained earlier,

Convinced that an optional protocol to the Convention raising the age of possible recruitment of persons into armed forces and their participation in hostilities will contribute effectively to the implementation of the principle that the best interests of the child are to be a primary consideration in all actions concerning children,

Noting that the twenty-sixth international Conference of the Red Cross and Red Crescent in December 1995 recommended, inter alia, that parties to conflict take every feasible step to ensure that children under the age of 18 years do not take part in hostilities,

Welcoming the unanimous adoption, in June 1999, of International Labour Organization Convention No. 182 on the Prohibition and Immediate Action for the Elimination of the Worst Forms of Child Labour, which prohibits, inter alia, forced or compulsory recruitment of children for use in armed conflict,

Condemning with the gravest concern the recruitment, training and use within and across national borders of children in hostilities by armed groups distinct from the armed forces of a State, and recognizing the responsibility of those who recruit, train and use children in this regard,

Recalling the obligation of each party to an armed conflict to abide by the provisions of international humanitarian law,

Stressing that this Protocol is without prejudice to the purposes and principles contained in the Charter of the United Nations, including Article 51, and relevant norms of humanitarian law,

Bearing in mind that conditions of peace and security based on full respect of the purposes and principles contained in the Charter and observance of applicable human rights instruments are indispensable for the full protection of children, in particular during armed conflicts and foreign occupation,

Recognizing the special needs of those children who are particularly vulnerable to recruitment or use in hostilities contrary to this Protocol owing to their economic or social status or gender,

Mindful of the necessity of taking into consideration the economic, social and political root causes of the involvement of children in armed conflicts,

Convinced of the need to strengthen international cooperation in the implementation of this Protocol, as well as the physical and psychosocial rehabilitation and social reintegration of children who are victims of armed conflict,

Encouraging the participation of the community and, in particular, children and child victims in the dissemination of informational and educational programmes concerning the implementation of the Protocol,

Have agreed as follows:

Article 1

States Parties shall take all feasible measures to ensure that members of their armed forces who have not attained the age of 18 years do not take a direct part in hostilities.

Article 2

States Parties shall ensure that persons who have not attained the age of 18 years are not compulsorily recruited into their armed forces.

Article 3

1. States Parties shall raise the minimum age for the voluntary recruitment of persons into their national armed forces from that set out in article 38, para-

graph 3, of the Convention on the Rights of the Child,1 taking account of the principles contained in that article and recognizing that under the Convention persons under 18 are entitled to special protection.

2. Each State Party shall deposit a binding declaration upon ratification of or accession to this Protocol that sets forth the minimum age at which it will permit voluntary recruitment into its national armed forces and a description of the safeguards that it has adopted to ensure that such recruitment is not forced or coerced.

3. States Parties that permit voluntary recruitment into their national armed forces under the age of 18 shall maintain safeguards to ensure, as a minimum, that:

(a) Such recruitment is genuinely voluntary;

(b) Such recruitment is done with the informed consent of the person's parents or legal guardians;

(c) Such persons are fully informed of the duties involved in such military service;

(d) Such persons provide reliable proof of age prior to acceptance into national military service.

4. Each State Party may strengthen its declaration at any time by notification to that effect addressed to the Secretary-General of the United Nations, who shall inform all States Parties. Such notification shall take effect on the date on which it is received by the Secretary-General.

5. The requirement to raise the age in paragraph 1 of the present article does not apply to schools operated by or under the control of the armed forces of the States Parties, in keeping with articles 28 and 29 of the Convention on the Rights of the Child.

Article 4

1. Armed groups that are distinct from the armed forces of a State should not, under any circumstances, recruit or use in hostilities persons under the age of 18 years.

2. States Parties shall take all feasible measures to prevent such recruitment and use, including the adoption of legal measures necessary to prohibit and criminalize such practices.

3. The application of the present article under this Protocol shall not affect the legal status of any party to an armed conflict.

Article 5

Nothing in the present Protocol shall be construed as precluding provisions in the law of a State Party or in international instruments and international humanitarian law that are more conducive to the realization of the rights of the child.

Article 6

1. Each State Party shall take all necessary legal, administrative and other measures to ensure the effective implementation and enforcement of the provisions of this Protocol within its jurisdiction.

2. States Parties undertake to make the principles and provisions of the present Protocol widely known and promoted by appropriate means, to adults and children alike.

3. States Parties shall take all feasible measures to ensure that persons within their jurisdiction recruited or used in hostilities contrary to this Protocol are demobilized or otherwise released from service. States Parties shall, when necessary, accord to these persons all appropriate assistance for their physical and psychological recovery and their social reintegration.

Article 7

1. States Parties shall cooperate in the implementation of the present Protocol, including in the prevention of any activity contrary to the Protocol and in the rehabilitation and social reintegration of persons who are victims of acts contrary to this Protocol, including through technical cooperation and financial assistance. Such assistance and cooperation will be undertaken in consultation with concerned States Parties and relevant international organizations.

2. States Parties in a position to do so shall provide such assistance through existing multilateral, bilateral or other programmes, or, inter alia, through a voluntary fund established in accordance with the rules of the General Assembly.

Article 8

1. Each State Party shall submit, within two years following the entry into force of the Protocol for that State Party, a report to the Committee on the Rights of the Child providing comprehensive information on the measures it has taken to implement the provisions of the Protocol, including the measures taken to implement the provisions on participation and recruitment.

2. Following the submission of the comprehensive report, each State Party shall include in the reports they submit to the Committee on the Rights of the Child, in accordance with article 44 of the Convention, any further information with respect to the implementation of the Protocol. Other States Parties to the Protocol shall submit a report every five years.

3. The Committee on the Rights of the Child may request from States Parties further information relevant to the implementation of this Protocol.

Article 9

1. The present Protocol is open for signature by any State that is a party to the Convention or has signed it.

2. The present Protocol is subject to ratification and is open to accession by any

State. Instruments of ratification or accession shall be deposited with the Secretary-General of the United Nations.

3. The Secretary-General, in his capacity as depositary of the Convention and the Protocol, shall inform all States Parties to the Convention and all States that have signed the Convention of each instrument of declaration pursuant to article 13.

Article 10

1. The present Protocol shall enter into force three months after the deposit of the tenth instrument of ratification or accession.

2. For each State ratifying the present Protocol or acceding to it after its entry into force, the present Protocol shall enter into force one month after the date of the deposit of its own instrument of ratification or accession.

Article 11

1. Any State Party may denounce the present Protocol at any time by written notification to the Secretary-General of the United Nations, who shall thereafter inform the other States Parties to the Convention and all States that have signed the Convention. The denunciation shall take effect one year after the date of receipt of the notification by the Secretary-General. If, however, on the expiry of that year the denouncing State Party is engaged in armed conflict, the denunciation shall not take effect before the end of the armed conflict.

2. Such a denunciation shall not have the effect of releasing the State Party from its obligations under the present Protocol in regard to any act that occurs prior to the date on which the denunciation becomes effective. Nor shall such a denunciation prejudice in any way the continued consideration of any matter that is already under consideration by the Committee prior to the date on which the denunciation becomes effective.

Article 12

1. Any State Party may propose an amendment and file it with the Secretary-General of the United Nations. The Secretary-General shall thereupon communicate the proposed amendment to States Parties, with a request that they indicate whether they favour a conference of States Parties for the purpose of considering and voting upon the proposals. In the event that, within four months from the date of such communication, at least one third of the States Parties favour such a conference, the Secretary-General shall convene the conference under the auspices of the United Nations. Any amendment adopted by a majority of States Parties present and voting at the conference shall be submitted to the General Assembly for approval.

2. An amendment adopted in accordance with paragraph 1 of the present article shall enter into force when it has been approved by the General Assembly of the United Nations and accepted by a two-thirds majority of States Parties.

3. When an amendment enters into force, it shall be binding on those States Parties that have accepted it, other States Parties still being bound by the provisions of the present Protocol and any earlier amendments that they have accepted.

Article 13

1. The present Protocol, of which the Arabic, Chinese, English, French, Russian and Spanish texts are equally authentic, shall be deposited in the archives of the United Nations.

2. The Secretary-General of the United Nations shall transmit certified copies of the present Protocol to all States Parties to the Convention and all States that have signed the Convention.

Appendix V

Optional Protocol to the Convention on the Rights of the Child on the sale of children, child prostitution and child pornography

(Adopted by the General Assembly of the United Nations on 25 May 2000)

The States Parties to the present Protocol,

Considering that, in order further to achieve the purposes of the Convention on the Rights of the Child and the implementation of its provisions, especially articles 1, 11, 21, 32, 33, 34, 35 and 36, it would be appropriate to extend the measures that States Parties should undertake in order to guarantee the protection of the child from the sale of children, child prostitution and child pornography,

Considering also that the Convention on the Rights of the Child recognizes the right of the child to be protected from economic exploitation and from performing any work that is likely to be hazardous or to interfere with the child's education, or to be harmful to the child's health or physical, mental, spiritual, moral or social development,

Gravely concerned at the significant and increasing international traffic of children for the purpose of the sale of children, child prostitution and child pornography,

Deeply concerned at the widespread and continuing practice of sex tourism, to which children are especially vulnerable, as it directly promotes the sale of children, child prostitution and child pornography,

Recognizing that a number of particularly vulnerable groups, including girl children, are at greater risk of sexual exploitation, and that girl children are disproportionately represented among the sexually exploited,

Concerned about the growing availability of child pornography on the Internet and other evolving technologies, and recalling the International Conference on Combating Child Pornography on the Internet (Vienna, 1999) and, in particular, its conclusion calling for the worldwide criminalization of the production, distribution, exportation, transmission, importation, intentional possession and advertising of child pornography, and stressing the importance of closer cooperation and partnership between Governments and the Internet industry,

Believing that the elimination of the sale of children, child prostitution and child pornography will be facilitated by adopting a holistic approach, addressing the contributing factors, including underdevelopment, poverty, economic disparities, inequitable socio-economic structure, dysfunctioning families, lack of education, urban-rural migration, gender discrimination, irresponsible adult sexual behaviour, harmful traditional practices, armed conflicts and trafficking of children,

Believing that efforts to raise public awareness are needed to reduce consumer demand for the sale of children, child prostitution and child pornography, and also believing in the importance of strengthening global partnership among all actors and of improving law enforcement at the national level,

Noting the provisions of international legal instruments relevant to the protection of children, including the Hague Convention on the Protection of Children and Cooperation with Respect to Inter-Country Adoption, the Hague Convention on the Civil Aspects of International Child Abduction, the Hague Convention on Jurisdiction, Applicable Law, Recognition, Enforcement and Cooperation in Respect of Parental Responsibility and Measures for the Protection of Children, and International Labour Organization Convention No. 182 on the Prohibition and Immediate Action for the Elimination of the Worst Forms of Child Labour,

Encouraged by the overwhelming support for the Convention on the Rights of the Child, demonstrating the widespread commitment that exists for the promotion and protection of the rights of the child,

Recognizing the importance of the implementation of the provisions of the Programme of Action for the Prevention of the Sale of Children, Child Prostitution and Child Pornography and the Declaration and Agenda for Action adopted at the World Congress against Commercial Sexual Exploitation of Children, held at Stockholm from 27 to 31 August 1996, and the other relevant decisions and recommendations of pertinent international bodies,

Taking due account of the importance of the traditions and cultural values of each people for the protection and harmonious development of the child,

Have agreed as follows:

Article 1

States Parties shall prohibit the sale of children, child prostitution and child pornography as provided for by the present Protocol.

Article 2

For the purpose of the present Protocol:

(a) Sale of children means any act or transaction whereby a child is transferred by any person or group of persons to another for remuneration or any other consideration;

(b) Child prostitution means the use of a child in sexual activities for remuneration or any other form of consideration;

(c) Child pornography means any representation, by whatever means, of a child engaged in real or simulated explicit sexual activities or any representation of the sexual parts of a child for primarily sexual purposes.

Article 3

1. Each State Party shall ensure that, as a minimum, the following acts and activities are fully covered under its criminal or penal law, whether these

offences are committed domestically or transnationally or on an individual or organized basis:

(a) In the context of sale of children as defined in article 2:

(i) The offering, delivering or accepting, by whatever means, a child for the purpose of:

a. Sexual exploitation of the child;

b. Transfer of organs of the child for profit;

c. Engagement of the child in forced labour;

(ii) Improperly inducing consent, as an intermediary, for the adoption of a child in violation of applicable international legal instruments on adoption;

(b) Offering, obtaining, procuring or providing a child for child prostitution, as defined in article 2;

(c) Producing, distributing, disseminating, importing, exporting, offering, selling or possessing for the above purposes child pornography as defined in article 2.

2. Subject to the provisions of a State Party's national law, the same shall apply to an attempt to commit any of these acts and to complicity or participation in any of these acts.

3. Each State Party shall make these offences punishable by appropriate penalties that take into account their grave nature.

4. Subject to the provisions of its national law, each State Party shall take measures, where appropriate, to establish the liability of legal persons for offences established in paragraph 1 of the present article. Subject to the legal principles of the State Party, this liability of legal persons may be criminal, civil or administrative.

5. States Parties shall take all appropriate legal and administrative measures to ensure that all persons involved in the adoption of a child act in conformity with applicable international legal instruments.

Article 4

1. Each State Party shall take such measures as may be necessary to establish its jurisdiction over the offences referred to in article 3, paragraph 1, when the offences are commited in its territory or on board a ship or aircraft registered in that State.

2. Each State Party may take such measures as may be necessary to establish its jurisdiction over the offences referred to in article 3, paragraph 1, in the following cases:

(a) When the alleged offender is a national of that State or a person who has his habitual residence in its territory;

(b) When the victim is a national of that State.

3. Each State Party shall also take such measures as may be necessary to establish its jurisdiction over the above-mentioned offences when the alleged offender is present in its territory and it does not extradite him or her to another State Party on the ground that the offence has been committed by one of its nationals.

4. This Protocol does not exclude any criminal jurisdiction exercised in accordance with internal law.

Article 5

1. The offences referred to in article 3, paragraph 1, shall be deemed to be included as extraditable offences in any extradition treaty existing between States Parties and shall be included as extraditable offences in every extradition treaty subsequently concluded between them, in accordance with the conditions set forth in those treaties.

2. If a State Party that makes extradition conditional on the existence of a treaty receives a request for extradition from another State Party with which it has no extradition treaty, it may consider this Protocol as a legal basis for extradition in respect of such offences. Extradition shall be subject to the conditions provided by the law of the requested State.

3. States Parties that do not make extradition conditional on the existence of a treaty shall recognize such offences as extraditable offences between themselves subject to the conditions provided by the law of the requested State.

4. Such offences shall be treated, for the purpose of extradition between States Parties, as if they had been committed not only in the place in which they occurred but also in the territories of the States required to establish their jurisdiction in accordance with article 4.

5. If an extradition request is made with respect to an offence described in article 3, paragraph 1, and if the requested State Party does not or will not extradite on the basis of the nationality of the offender, that State shall take suitable measures to submit the case to its competent authorities for the purpose of prosecution.

Article 6

1. States Parties shall afford one another the greatest measure of assistance in connection with investigations or criminal or extradition proceedings brought in respect of the offences set forth in article 3, paragraph 1, including assistance in obtaining evidence at their disposal necessary for the proceedings.

2. States Parties shall carry out their obligations under paragraph 1 of the present article in conformity with any treaties or other arrangements on mutual legal assistance that may exist between them. In the absence of such treaties or arrangements, States Parties shall afford one another assistance in accordance with their domestic law.

Article 7

States Parties shall, subject to the provisions of their national law:
(a) Take measures to provide for the seizure and confiscation, as appropriate, of:
(i) Goods such as materials, assets and other instrumentalities used to commit or facilitate offences under the present protocol;
(ii) Proceeds derived from such offences;

(b) Execute requests from another State Party for seizure or confiscation of goods or proceeds referred to in subparagraph (a) (i);
(c) Take measures aimed at closing, on a temporary or definitive basis, premises used to commit such offences.

Article 8

1. States Parties shall adopt appropriate measures to protect the rights and interests of child victims of the practices prohibited under the present Protocol at all stages of the criminal justice process, in particular by:
(a) Recognizing the vulnerability of child victims and adapting procedures to recognize their special needs, including their special needs as witnesses;
(b) Informing child victims of their rights, their role and the scope, timing and progress of the proceedings and of the disposition of their cases;
(c) Allowing the views, needs and concerns of child victims to be presented and considered in proceedings where their personal interests are affected, in a manner consistent with the procedural rules of national law;
(d) Providing appropriate support services to child victims throughout the legal process;
(e) Protecting, as appropriate, the privacy and identity of child victims and taking measures in accordance with national law to avoid the inappropriate dissemination of information that could lead to the identification of child victims;
(f) Providing, in appropriate cases, for the safety of child victims, as well as that of their families and witnesses on their behalf, from intimidation and retaliation;
(g) Avoiding unnecessary delay in the disposition of cases and the execution of orders or decrees granting compensation to child victims.

2. States Parties shall ensure that uncertainty as to the actual age of the victim shall not prevent the initiation of criminal investigations, including investigations aimed at establishing the age of the victim.

3. States Parties shall ensure that, in the treatment by the criminal justice system of children who are victims of the offences described in the present Protocol, the best interest of the child shall be a primary consideration.

4. States Parties shall take measures to ensure appropriate training, in particular legal and psychological training, for the persons who work with victims of the offences prohibited under the present Protocol.

5. States Parties shall, in appropriate cases, adopt measures in order to protect the safety and integrity of those persons and/or organizations involved in the prevention and/or protection and rehabilitation of victims of such offences.

6. Nothing in the present article shall be construed as prejudicial to or inconsistent with the rights of the accused to a fair and impartial trial.

Article 9

1. States Parties shall adopt or strengthen, implement and disseminate laws, administrative measures, social policies and programmes to prevent the offences

referred to in the present Protocol. Particular attention shall be given to protect children who are especially vulnerable to these practices.

2. States Parties shall promote awareness in the public at large, including children, through information by all appropriate means, education and training, about the preventive measures and harmful effects of the offences referred to in the present Protocol. In fulfilling their obligations under this article, States Parties shall encourage the participation of the community and, in particular, children and child victims, in such information and education and training programmes, including at the international level.

3. States Parties shall take all feasible measures with the aim of ensuring all appropriate assistance to victims of such offences, including their full social reintegration and their full physical and psychological recovery.

4. States Parties shall ensure that all child victims of the offences described in the present Protocol have access to adequate procedures to seek, without discrimination, compensation for damages from those legally responsible.

5. States Parties shall take appropriate measures aimed at effectively prohibiting the production and dissemination of material advertising the offences described in the present Protocol.

Article 10

1. States Parties shall take all necessary steps to strengthen international cooperation by multilateral, regional and bilateral arrangements for the prevention, detection, investigation, prosecution and punishment of those responsible for acts involving the sale of children, child prostitution, child pornography and child sex tourism. States Parties shall also promote international cooperation and coordination between their authorities, national and international non-governmental organizations and international organizations.

2. States Parties shall promote international cooperation to assist child victims in their physical and psychological recovery, social reintegration and repatriation.

3. States Parties shall promote the strengthening of international cooperation in order to address the root causes, such as poverty and underdevelopment, contributing to the vulnerability of children to the sale of children, child prostitution, child pornography and child sex tourism.

4. States Parties in a position to do so shall provide financial, technical or other assistance through existing multilateral, regional, bilateral or other programmes.

Article 11

Nothing in the present Protocol shall affect any provisions that are more conducive to the realization of the rights of the child and that may be contained in:

(a) The law of a State Party;

(b) International law in force for that State.

Article 12

1. Each State Party shall submit, within two years following the entry into force of the Protocol for that State Party, a report to the Committee on the Rights of the Child providing comprehensive information on the measures it has taken to implement the provisions of the Protocol.

2. Following the submission of the comprehensive report, each State Party shall include in the reports they submit to the Committee on the Rights of the Child, in accordance with article 44 of the Convention, any further information with respect to the implementation of the Protocol. Other States Parties to the Protocol shall submit a report every five years.

3. The Committee on the Rights of the Child may request from States Parties further information relevant to the implementation of this Protocol.

Article 13

1. The present Protocol is open for signature by any State that is a party to the Convention or has signed it.

2. The present Protocol is subject to ratification and is open to accession by any State that is a party to the Convention or has signed it. Instruments of ratification or accession shall be deposited with the Secretary-General of the United Nations.

Article 14

1. The present Protocol shall enter into force three months after the deposit of the tenth instrument of ratification or accession.

2. For each State ratifying the present Protocol or acceding to it after its entry into force, the present Protocol shall enter into force one month after the date of the deposit of its own instrument of ratification or accession.

Article 15

1. Any State Party may denounce the present Protocol at any time by written notification to the Secretary-General of the United Nations, who shall thereafter inform the other States Parties to the Convention and all States that have signed the Convention. The denunciation shall take effect one year after the date of receipt of the notification by the Secretary-General of the United Nations.

2. Such a denunciation shall not have the effect of releasing the State Party from its obligations under this Protocol in regard to any offence that occurs prior to the date on which the denunciation becomes effective. Nor shall such a denunciation prejudice in any way the continued consideration of any matter that is already under consideration by the Committee prior to the date on which the denunciation becomes effective.

Article 16

1. Any State Party may propose an amendment and file it with the Secretary-General of the United Nations. The Secretary-General shall thereupon communi-

cate the proposed amendment to States Parties, with a request that they indicate whether they favour a conference of States Parties for the purpose of considering and voting upon the proposals. In the event that, within four months from the date of such communication, at least one third of the States Parties favour such a conference, the Secretary-General shall convene the conference under the auspices of the United Nations. Any amendment adopted by a majority of States Parties present and voting at the conference shall be submitted to the General Assembly for approval.

2. An amendment adopted in accordance with paragraph 1 of the present article shall enter into force when it has been approved by the General Assembly of the United Nations and accepted by a two-thirds majority of States Parties.

3. When an amendment enters into force, it shall be binding on those States Parties that have accepted it, other States Parties still being bound by the provisions of the present Protocol and any earlier amendments that they have accepted.

Article 17

1. The present Protocol, of which the Arabic, Chinese, English, French, Russian and Spanish texts are equally authentic, shall be deposited in the archives of the United Nations.

2. The Secretary-General of the United Nations shall transmit certified copies of the present Protocol to all States Parties to the Convention and all States that have signed the Convention.

SELECTED BIBLIOGRAPHY

Adams, P. e.a., *Children's rights. Towards the liberation of the Child*, New York, Praeger, 1972.

Alston, F., Parker, S., Seymour, J. (eds.), *Children, Rights and the Law,* Oxford, Clarendon Press, 1992.

Aries, Ph., *L'enfant et la vie familiale sous l'ancien régime*, Paris, Librairie Plon, 1960.

Bada, A., *The "working children and young people" join forces to improve their living conditions*, in: Verhellen, E. (ed.), Understanding children's rights, Ghent Papers on Children's Rights, N° 3, Ghent, Children's Rights Centre, 1998, pp. 255-260.

Badinter, E., *L'amour en plus. Histoire de l'amour maternel*, Paris, Flammarion, 1980.

Boucaud, P., *The Council Europe and child welfare: The need for a European convention on children's rights*, Strasbourg, Council of Europe, Directorate of Human Rights, Human rights files N°10, 1989.

Boulding, E., *Children's rights and the wheel of life*, New Brunswick, Transaction Books, 1979.

Buquicchio-de Boer, *Les enfants et la Convention européenne des Droits de l'Homme: Etude de la jurisprudence de la Commission et de la Cour européennes des Droits de l'Homme*, Strasbourg, Conseil de l'Europe, C.D.D.H., 87.29F, le 22 septembre 1987 (mise á jour en mai 1990).

Castillo, M., *Les droits des enfants dans la Communauté*, Florence, Institut Universitaire Européen, 1989.

Cattrijsse, L., *CRUN - Children's rights Universities Network - Introduction*, in: Verhellen, E. (ed.), Understanding children's rights, Ghent papers on Children's Rights, N° 5, Ghent, Children's Rights Centre, 1999, pp. 133-138.

Cattrijsse, L., *Children's rights and education. The right TO, IN and THROUGH education: three interrelated imperatives*, in: Verhellen, E.(ed.), Understanding children's rights, Ghent papers on Children's Rights, N° 5, Ghent, Children's Rights Centre, 1999, pp. 574-593.

Cohen, H., *Equal rights for children*, Littlefield, Adams & Co, Towota, 1980.

Council of Europe, *Texts drawn-up by the Council of Europe in the field of childhood policies: Bibliography*, Strasbourg, C.D.P.S. III.8 (92) 6, revised, 19 November, 1992.

Council of Europe, *Texts drawn-up by the Council of Europe in the field of childhood policies: Resolutions, Recommendations of the Committee of Ministers*, Strasbourg, C.D.P.S. III.8 (92) 10, 7 December, 1992.

Council of Europe, *Recommendations of the Parlementary Assembly in the field of childhood policies*, Strasbourg, C.D.P.S. III.8 (92) 8, 25 June, 1992.

Cnudde, H., *What do you think? Children reporting on children's rights*, in: Verhellen, E. (ed.), Understanding children's rights, Ghent papers on Children's Rights, N° 5, Ghent, Children's Rights Centre, 1999, pp. 221-232.

Dasberg, L., *Grootbrengen door kleinhouden als historisch verschijnsel*, Meppel, Boom, 1986, elfde druk.

De Mause, L., *The history of childhood*, New York, Psychohistory Press, 1974.

De Paepe, M., *Understanding the history of childhood from the perspective of educationalization*, in: Verhellen, E. (ed.), Understanding children's rights, Ghent papers on Children's Rights, N° 3, Ghent, Children's Rights Centre, 1998, pp. 39-66.

Dettrick, S. (ed.), *The United Nations Convention on the Rights of the Child. A Guide to the "Travaux Préparatoires"*, Dordrecht, Martinus Nijhoff, 1992.

Droogleever Fortuyn, M., De Langen, M. (eds.), *Towards the realization of human rights of children*, Amsterdam, DCI-The Netherlands, 1992.

Farson, R., *Birth-rights*, New York, Macmillan, 1974.

Flekkóy, M.C., *A Voice for Children*, London, Jessica Kingsley, 1991.

Flekkóy, M.G., *Children's Rights: reflections on and consequences of the use of developmental psychology in working for the interests of children. The Norwegian, Ombudsman for Children: A practical experience*, Ghent, Children's Rights Centre, 1993.

Freeman, M., Veerman, P.E. (eds.), *The Ideologies of Children's Rights*, Dordrecht, Martinus Nijhoff, 1992.

Freeman, M., *The moral status of children: Essays on the rights of the child*, Dordrecht, Martinus Nijhoff, 1997.

Gottlieb, D. (ed.), *Children's liberation*, Englewood Cliffs, Prentice-Hall, 1973.

Gröner, L., *Report on problems of children in the European Community*, European Parliament, 19 June 1991. *Resolution on the problems of children in the European Community*, E.P., 13 December 1991.

Gross, B., Gross, R. (eds.), *The children's rights movement. Overcoming the oppression of young people*, New York, Anchor Press-Doubleday, 1977.

Hanson, K., *Draft of a source book on children's rights*, in: Verhellen, E. (ed.), Understanding children's rights, Ghent papers on Children's Rights, N° 5, Ghent, Children's Rights Centre, 1999, pp. 432-441.

Hart, R., *Children's participation. From tokenism to citizenship*, Florence, UNICEF International Child Development Centre, Spedale Degli Innocenti, 1992.

Hart, R., *Children's participation, The theory and practice of involving young citizens in community development and environmental care*, London, Earthscan, 1997.

Haeck, Y., Goedertier, G., *The reporting procedure of the Convention on the rights of the child*, in: Verhellen, E.(ed.) Understanding children's rights, Ghent papers on Children's Rights, N° 5, Ghent, Children's Rights Centre, 1999, pp. 359-409.

Holt, J., *Escape from childhood. The needs and rights of children*, New York, Ballantine, 1974.

Hodgkin, R., Newell, P., *The implementation handbook for the Convention on the Rights of the Child*, New York, Unicef, 1998.

Jaffé, Ph., *Competence? Now really!* in: Verhellen, E., (ed.), Understanding children's rights, Ghent papers on children's rights, N° 5, Ghent, Children's Rights Centre, 1999, pp. 37-46.

James, A., Prout, A., *Constructing and reconstructing childhood*, Basington, Falmer, 1990.

Jenks, C. (ed.), *The sociology of childhood: essential readings*, Hampshire, Gregg revivals, 1992.

Knutsonn, K., *Children: Noble causes or worthy citizens*, Aldershot, Arena-Ashgate, 1997.

Lopatka, A., *Convention on the rights of the child: history, content, impact*, in: Verhellen, E. (ed.), Understanding children's rights, Ghent papers on childrens rights, N° 5, Ghent, Children's Rights Centre, 1999, pp. 343-358.

Mas, E., *The protection of minors under the European Convention on Human Rights: Analysis of Case Law*, I.M.C.L. and C.I.A.S. Conference, Law relating to minors and minor's rights, Strasbourg, Council of Europe, H (90) 7, 20 June 1990.

Mendel, C., *Pour décoloniser l'enfant*, Paris, Payot, 1971.

Mortier, F., *Rationality and competence to decide in children*, in: Verhellen, E. (ed.), Understanding children's rights, Ghent papers on Children's Rights, N° 3, Ghent, Children's Rights Centre, 1998, pp. 79-100.

Nieuwenhuys, O., *Children's lifeworlds: Gender, welfare and labour in the developing world*, London/New York, Routledge, 1994.

Pas, W., Vandaele, A., *International human rights treaties and their relation with national law: monism, dualism and the self-executing force character of human rights*, in: Verhellen, E. (ed.), Understanding children's rights, Ghent papers on Children's Rights, N° 5, Ghent, Children's Rights Centre, 1999, pp. 285-302.

Pollock, L., *Forgotten children: Parent-child relations from 1500-1900*, Cambridge, University Press,1983.

Qvortrup, J., *Childhood as a Social Phenomenon. An Introduction to a Series of National Reports*, Eurosocial Report 36/1990, Vienna, European Centre, 1990.

Qvortrup, J., Bardy, M, Sigritta, G., Wintersberger, H., (eds.), *Childhood matters*, Aldershot, Aveburry, 1994.

Raes, K., *Children's rights and modern culture, The politics of juridification and its limits*, in: Verhellen, E.(ed.), Understanding children's rights, Ghent papers on Children's Rights, N° 2, Ghent, Children's Rights Centre, 1997, pp. 9-26.

Skolnick, A.S., *The intimate environment. Exploring marriage and the family*, Boston/Toronto, Little Brown and Company, 1983.

Starkey, H. (ed.), *The challenge of Human Rights education*, Strasbourg, Council of Europe, 1991.

Swift, A., *Working children get organised. An introduction to working children's organisations*, London, International Save the Children Alliance, 1999.

Symonides, J., *Unesco and education for human rights*, in: Verhellen, E. (ed.), Understanding children's rights, Ghent papers on Children's Rights, N° 3, Ghent, Children's Rights Centre, 1998, pp. 703-718.

Theytaz-Bergman, L., *Networking within the NGO Community: The NGO Group for the Convention on the Rights of the Child*, in: Verhellen, E. (ed.), Understanding children's rights, Ghent papers on Children's Rights, N° 3, Ghent, Children's Rights Centre, 1998, pp. 189-192.

Van Bueren, G., (ed.), *The international law on the rights of the child*, Dordrecht, Martinus Nijhoff, 1995.

Vandekerckhove, A., *A commissioner for children in the Flemish Community in Belgium*, in: Verhellen, E. (ed.), Understanding children's rights, Ghent papers on Children's Rights, N° 5, Ghent, Children's Rights Centre, 1999, pp. 93-104.

Veerman, P.E., *The rights of the child and the changing image of childhood*, Dordrecht, Martinus Nijhof, 1992.

Verhellen, E., Spiesschaert, F. (eds.), *Ombudswork for children*, Leuven/Amersfoort, Acco, 1989.

Verhellen, E., Spiesschaert, F. (eds.), *Children's Rights: Monitoring Issues*, Gent, Mys & Breesch, 1994.

Verhellen, E. (ed.), *Monitoring Children's Rights*, Kluwer Law International, The Hague, 1996.

Verhellen, E., *Children's rights: Education and academic responsibilities*, in: Jaffé, Ph. (ed.), Changing Mentalities, Implementing the United Nations Convention on the Rights of the Child, Ghent papers on Children's Rights, N° 4, Ghent, Children's Rights Centre, 1998, pp. 97-124.

Verhellen, E. (ed.), *Understanding Children's Rights, Collected papers at the International Interdisplinary Courses on Children's Rights*, University of Ghent (academic years 1996-2000), Ghent, Children's Rights Centre, 1996, 1997, 1998, 1999, 2000).

Worsfold, V., *A philosophical justification for children's rights*, Harvard Educational Review, vol. 44, n° 1, 1974, pp. 142-157.

Wringe, C., *Children's rights. A philosophical study*, London, Routledge and Kegan Paul, 1981.